CONFIDENTIALITY AND THE LAW

CONFIDENTIALITY AND THE LAW

EDITED BY

LINDA CLARKE

B.A.(Hons), LL.B.(Cantab.)

Lecturer in Law

University of Sussex

|L|L|P|

LONDON NEW YORK HAMBURG HONG KONG

LLOYD'S OF LONDON PRESS LTD.

1990

Lloyd's of London Press Ltd.
Legal Publishing and Conferences Division
One Singer Street, London EC2A 4LQ
Great Britain

USA AND CANADA
Lloyd's of London Press Inc.
Suite 308, 611 Broadway,
New York, NY 10012, USA

GERMANY
Lloyd's of London Press GmbH
59 Ehrenbergstrasse, 2000 Hamburg 50
Germany

SOUTH-EAST ASIA
Lloyd's of London Press (Far East) Ltd.
Room 1101, Hollywood Centre
233 Hollywood Road
Hong Kong

British Library Cataloguing in Publication Data
Confidentiality and the law.
1. England. Confidential information. Misuse. Law
I. Clarke, Linda
344.20633

ISBN 1–85044–323–8

Text set 11 on 13 pt Linotron 202 Sabon by
BP Integraphics Ltd, Bath, Avon
Printed in Great Britain by
Bookcraft Ltd
Midsomer Norton

PREFACE

Confidentiality is a multi-faceted legal issue involving aspects of both public and private law, criminal and civil. Its origins lie in the equitable jurisdiction of the Chancery Division to grant injunctions to prevent the infringement of legal or equitable rights. The willingness of the courts to protect confidences may arise from the nature of the relationship between the parties—husband and wife, employer and employee, doctor and patient—or may be based in the terms of a contract, express or implied. English law has no express principle in favour of freedom of expression, such as can be found in Article 10 of the European Convention on Human Rights, and, instead, this becomes part of the judicial balancing act referred to by Mr Justice Scott in his introduction; the judges, in exercising their discretion, take account of "the public interest" which includes the public interest in the free exchange of ideas and information.

The essays in this collection aim to question whether the balance between such competing rights is being struck correctly: does the law, through the doctrine of breach of confidence, value contractual and property rights above the right to freedom of expression, or does the doctrine fail to protect adequately other rights, such as privacy? Topical areas such as banking, employment, access to medical records and computer hacking are discussed, as is the conceptual problem of whether information can be viewed as a form of property in itself. It is hoped that this work will improve understanding of how the law has developed in the past, and to suggest ways in which it may continue to develop in the future.

This book originated in a conference held in Colchester in the winter of 1988. At the time, the *Spycatcher* litigation was progressing through the courts and the conference provoked great interest and enthusiasm amongst audience and contributors alike; this book is the final result of that interest. Not all the contributors took part in the original conference, and those that did have considerably revised their chapters in the light of later developments. We were fortunate enough to have the Conference opened by Mr Justice Scott, who gave the original High Court judgment in *Spycatcher*, subsequently upheld by the House of Lords, and he has been kind enough to write an Introduction to this volume. I would like to thank all the contributors for the considerable time and effort which they have devoted to this project, and in particular Professor Norman Palmer, who had the initial idea for both conference and book. Finally, I would like to express my gratitude to Lloyd's of London Press for their encouragement and enthusiasm, and to Harriet, but for whose arrival in the world I might have been able to write a chapter myself.

September 1990 LINDA CLARKE

CONTENTS

CONTRIBUTORS

COLIN MUNRO is Professor of Constitutional Law in the University of Edinburgh, having previously held appointments at the Universities of Birmingham, Durham, Essex and Manchester. He is also Assistant Editor of *Public Law*. His books include *Television, Censorship and the Law* (Gower, 1979) and *Studies in Constitutional Law* (Butterworths, 1987).

ROBERT LEE is Director of Education at Wilde-Sapte Solicitors, a large commercial practice based in the City of London. Prior to joining Wilde-Sapte, he was a Lecturer and senior Tutor at the University of Lancaster. He is author of a number of books on both public law and medical law, and lectures widely on the latter topic. He is also an Honorary Fellow in the Centre for Science Studies and Science Policy at the University of Lancaster.

MARK THOMPSON is a lecturer in law at Leicester University, having previously held lectureships at the Universities of Keele and Essex. He is General Editor of the *Conveyancing Solutions* series (Sweet and Maxwell) and has written books on *Co-ownership*, and *The Investigation and Proof of Title*. He acted as consultant to the Law Commission during the production of the Working Papers on *Bain* v. *Fothergill* and the *Passing of Risk*.

NORMAN PALMER is Professor of English Law at the University of Southampton and a practising barrister, formerly having held Chairs at the Universities of Reading and Essex. He is the author of *Bailment* (1979) and the co-editor of Emden's *Construction Law* (1990) and *Crossley Vaines on Personal Property* (1973).

He is also a contributor to the 4th edition of Halsbury's *Laws of England*. He is the Director of the International Cultural Property Society, and the Editor of the *International Journal of Cultural Property*. He is a former member of the Tasmanian Law Reform Commission.

BRIAN NAPIER is Digital Professor of Information Technology Law at the Centre for Commercial Law Studies, Queen Mary and Westfield College, University of London, having previously been a Lecturer at the University of Cambridge and Fellow of Queen's College. He is the joint editor of *Harvey on Industrial Relations and Employment Law*, and the joint author of *Butterworth's Employment Law Guide* (1990). He was Visiting Professor at the University of Paris 1 and 2 in 1980–1981, and has worked as an expert for the International Labour Office on the revision of labour legislation in various African states.

JEFFREY CHAPMAN is a barrister, and worked at the Law Commission on diverse criminal law projects, including the Working Paper and Report on *Computer Misuse*.

JENNIFER STUCKEY-CLARKE is a Lecturer in Intellectual Property Law and the Principles of Equity at the University of Sydney. She also acts as consultant to the Intellectual Property Section of Blake, Dawson Waldron (Solicitors) Sydney.

TABLE OF CASES

TABLE OF LEGISLATION, ETC

INTRODUCTION

One of the most important functions of the civil law is to identify the points at which a person can complain about and obtain redress to remedy the acts or omissions of another person. Cases of negligence and of nuisance provide obvious and familiar examples of this function of the law. Judges who try these cases are involved in the striking of a balance between rival interests. On one side of the balance will be the interests of the plaintiff, and of others in similar circumstances, not to be injured and annoyed or interfered with by the acts or omissions complained of. On the other side of the balance will lie the interests of the defendant, and of others like him who want to pursue their lives or their businesses or their hobbies as they think fit without being hampered or restrained by consideration for the interests of others. The competing interests of the plaintiff and the defendant will be private interests. But into the balance will go public interests as well. There is a general public interest that people should not be placed in physical danger by the activities of others. There is a general public interest that people in the quiet of their homes should not be disturbed by excessive noise or unpleasant smells or by undue harassment. But there is a public interest, too, that the conduct of business, the flow of traffic, the pursuit of a profession, the enjoyment of sport, should not be made impracticable by imposing on the shoulders of entrepreneurs, of motorists, of professionals or of sportsmen an excessively onerous burden of legal responsibility. There is a balance to be struck and, save where statute applies, the balance must be struck by the judges who try the cases. In striking this balance judges will be guided by case law but, nonetheless, can reflect in their judgments the changing requirements of an ever evolving society.

I have mentioned these truisms, regarding negligence and nuisance, with which every law student will be familiar, because of the strong analogy between the approach in negligence and nuisance cases and the approach in cases in which the law of confidentiality must be applied.

There has been over the last few years a spate of cases involving the law of confidentiality. The cases have covered a very wide variety of subjects. Some have concerned confidential disclosures between spouses, the so-called secrets of the marriage bed (*Argyll* v. *Argyll*), some the secrets of government (*Attorney-General* v. *Guardian Newspapers* (*No.* 2)), some the duty of a doctor to his patient (*W.* v. *Egdell*), others the results of over-zealous investigative journalism (*Francome* v. *Mirror Group Newspapers*). In some cases duties of confidentiality have been spelled out of contract. But in most cases the duties have been treated as imposed by the general law in order to restrain unconscionable conduct, and it is well established that a contractual source is no more necessary for obligations of confidence than it is for duties of care.

The law of confidentiality, like the law of negligence and the law of nuisance, requires a balance to be struck. The balance will, on both sides, involve public and private interests. The newspapers that wanted to publish extracts from *Spycatcher* had private commercial interests in doing so. But there was also a public interest in freedom of speech. On the other side there was a public interest in the protection of the secrets of the security service (no private interest since the litigant was the Government). In the *Francome* case, the plaintiff had a private interest in maintaining the privacy of his telephone conversations but, ranged on the same side, there was a public interest that private telephone conversations should not be the subject of eavesdropping. On the other side, the *Daily Mirror* could rely, in aid of its own private interest, on the public interest in the disclosure of alleged wrongdoing. These are examples to make the point that every case where the law of confidentiality is invoked requires the judge to strike a balance between competing interests.

The law of confidentiality has, therefore, an inherent flexibility, similar to that of negligence or of nuisance, capable of enabling it to keep pace with changing social and economic circumstances and to cater for the needs and changing requirements of the times.

These introductory remarks are prompted, at least in part, by the recent Court of Appeal decision in *Kaye* v. *Robertson* (*The Times* of 21 March 1990). The Court of Appeal held that a trespassing journalist who took unauthorised photographs of the plaintiff in his hospital bed, could not be restrained by injunction from publishing the photographs in a daily newspaper. One of the judges commented on "... the failure of ... the common law of England ... to protect in an effective way the personal privacy of individual citizens". Another said that a right to privacy "had so long disregarded ... that it could be recognised now only by the legislature". But nowhere, in the report of the judgments, was there any mention of the law of confidentiality. Why not? It is not essential to a cause of action based on the law of confidentiality that the information or material should have been specifically disclosed or confided by a confider. Lord Griffiths made that point in his speech in the *Spycatcher* case. What difference should the law of confidentiality draw between a telephone eavesdropper (the *Francome* case) and a Peeping Tom who reports to a newspaper what he has seen, or between the Peeping Tom and an investigative journalist with a long-range telephoto lens? Why should not a developing law of confidentiality be capable of applying to the latter two situations as well as to the first? Why should not the balance to which I have referred be struck into whichever of these three categories the case falls?

It is my belief that the law of confidentiality can, in conjunction with the law of trespass and the law of nuisance, go a long way to remedy the alleged absence of a right to privacy under English law. Whether the law of confidentiality will develop so as to do so remains to be seen. If it is to do so, a proper understanding of its nature and its potential is an essential preliminary. For this reason I particularly welcome the publication of the essays contained in this book. The careful examination of various aspects of the law of confidentiality that the essays contain will provide a valuable aid to practitioners in understanding and dealing with issues of confidentiality. The essays will, also, assist judges in the development of this important area of judge-made law.

September 1990 RICHARD SCOTT

CHAPTER 1

CONFIDENCE IN GOVERNMENT

The *Spycatcher* saga contained all the necessary ingredients to ensure great public interest, and as a result, the capacity of the law of confidence to protect government information has probably become its best known feature. The proposition that government information could, in appropriate circumstances, be the object of a legally enforceable confidence, was previously neither indisputable nor uncontroversial. However, earlier case law had supported the proposition, and the recent decision of the House of Lords must be taken to settle the matter. The public lawyer's interest in this branch of law is apt to be strengthened rather than extinguished by that affirmation, for it merely raises a host of other issues. One obvious question is whether the same principles apply to the action for breach of confidence when government information is involved. Another interesting question is why governments have relied on the law of confidence in seeking to prevent disclosures of information about government, when another part of the law, apparently more suited to the purpose, was at hand.

CONCEPTUAL CONFUSIONS

As is well known, the action for breach of confidence developed in the nineteenth and early twentieth centuries, predominantly in commercial spheres.[1] In 1965, however, there was a case of a quite different kind, *Duchess of Argyll* v. *Duke of Argyll*.[2] The Duke's third wife, Margaret, from whom he had recently

1. See generally Law Com. No. 110 (1981), *Breach of Confidence*; Francis Gurry, *Breach of Confidence* (1984); G. Jones, "Restitution of Benefits Obtained in Breach of Another's Confidence" (1970) 86 L.Q.R. 463.
2. [1967] Ch. 302.

been divorced, obtained an injunction to prevent him from revealing in a Sunday newspaper further details of her life with (and apart from) him, on the ground that these were marital confidences which the law would protect. His former wife had already published her account in another Sunday newspaper, but the judge (Ungoed-Thomas J.) overlooked that, on the view that the Duke's articles were of a different order of perfidy.

In that decision, with its confirmation that the law would protect personal confidences, the germ of some protection for privacy could be discerned. Certainly, the Younger Committee, which was set up in 1970 to examine whether the law should afford greater protection to privacy, not only perceived the connection but seized on it with some relief. The committee declined to recommend the enactment of a general right of privacy, but proposed a number of limited reforms.[3] They considered that the action for breach of confidence could provide "much greater protection of privacy than is generally realised,"[4] and it was on their proposal that the law of confidence was referred to the Law Commission, resulting in their Report in 1981, which recommended the creation of a new statutory tort.[5]

In fact, the Younger Committee's hopes were, to a large extent, misplaced. "Confidentiality" and "privacy" are distinct concepts, and a proper analysis would have demonstrated that the action for breach of confidence would at best be an inadequate remedy for breaches of privacy.[6]

3. Report of the Committee on Privacy, Cmnd. 5012 (1972).

4. *Ibid.*, para. 630.

5. Law Com. No. 110 (1981), *Breach of Confidence*.

6. This is not the place to develop this argument fully. In brief, the point is that many breaches of what is conceived of as privacy (for example, snooping, "doorstepping", unsolicited calls, "false light" cases, and appropriation of the plaintiff's name or likeness) do not typically involve any information imparted in confidence, and disclosures of embarrassing facts (such as a criminal record or treatment in a mental hospital) are sometimes brought about by breaches of confidence, but often not. See generally R. Wacks, *The Protection of Privacy* (1980); G. Dworkin, "Privacy and the Law", in J.B. Young (ed.), *Privacy* (1978). For a more optimistic view of the capacity of the law of confidence to remedy breaches of privacy, see Chapter 4 in this volume and also Mark Thompson's "Breach of Confidence and the Protection of Privacy in English Law" (1985) 6 *Journal of Media Law and Practice* 5. However, the Law Commission warned that: "It is important to bear in mind the essentially different nature of the two kinds of right" : Law Com. No. 110 (1981), para. 2.4.

The committee had fallen prey to conceptual confusion, which is rife in this area. If it is important for "confidentiality" and "privacy" to be carefully distinguished, then it is equally necessary to distinguish a third concept, "secrecy", which is not the same as either "confidentiality" or "privacy". "Secret" matters are not necessarily "private", and privacy is not only concerned with keeping secrets.[7]

"Confidentiality", in its legal sense, arises when information which has the necessary quality of confidence about it has been imparted in circumstances importing an obligation of confidence.[8] "Secrecy", as a concept of English law, arises from the operation of the Official Secrets Acts 1911–1989. It is a *narrower* legal category than "confidentiality", inasmuch as it applies only to information obtained, or to which a person has had access, owing to his position as one holding, or who has held, office under the Crown or who is or has been a government contractor or someone in his employ. However, the scope for relevant information to fall within this category is *wider*, in so far as it need not have been transmitted as part of a confidential relationship.

Thus, the categories of legally confidential information and legally secret information overlap, but are by no means co-extensive. The government's failure to distinguish these legal categories carefully has contributed to a dangerous widening of the law of confidence. Moreover, its deployment of an inappropriate legal remedy in its attempts to prevent the publication of the book *Spycatcher* has merely resulted in its world-wide embarrassment and a cost to the taxpayer of several million pounds. To see how these results have come to pass, it is necessary to review the development of the law of confidence regarding government information, and consider also the law which was not used, the law concerning official secrecy.

THE EARLIER CASE LAW

The *Argyll* case, even if it involved a dramatic extension of the law of confidence beyond its commercial origins, was at least

7. See C. J. Friedrich, "Secrecy versus Privacy: The Democratic Dilemma", in J. R. Pennock and J. W. Chapman (eds.), *Privacy* (*Nomos XIII*) (1971).

8. This is based on the well-known formulation of principles by Megarry J. in *Coco* v. *A. N. Clark (Engineers) Ltd.* [1969] R.P.C. 41 at p. 47.

still concerned with *private* rights. The conception of a *public* right to keep something confidential first surfaced in the *Crossman Diaries* case in 1975.[9]

Richard Crossman, a Cabinet Minister in the Wilson governments from 1964 to 1970, kept diaries of his political life and, aspiring to be the Bagehot of his age, had the avowed purpose of opening up the secret places of government. In 1974, when Crossman died, he had finished editing the first volume of his diaries, describing events between 1964 and 1966. Nothing would have deterred him from proceeding to publication, so his literary executors felt honour-bound to do the same. There was besides a contract with the *Sunday Times*, which in Harold Evans had a campaigning editor who was already a veteran of the legal battles on thalidomide.[10] Meanwhile, the 1974 general elections had brought Mr Wilson back at the head of a Labour government which comprised many of the same politicians who had held office 10 years earlier. Whatever the politicians may have thought about it, the Cabinet Secretary of the time, Sir John Hunt, was determined to restrain publication of the diaries in their unexpurgated form, and asked for deletions to be made in line with what he called his "parameters", formulations which purported to represent past practice. The newspaper began publishing extracts prior to the publication of the book, and for some weeks played a cat-and-mouse game with the Cabinet Secretary, by agreeing to some but not all of his requests and by giving him insufficient time for full consideration of the extracts before they went to press. The *Sunday Times* completed the series which it intended, having published 85,000 words from the first volume, and leaving the Cabinet Secretary's "parameters" in ruins. It was only then that the Treasury Solicitor could brook no more, and instructed the Attorney-General to seek injunctions to stop the publication of the book or further publication of extracts in the newspaper.

But what was the Attorney-General's cause of action? Of course, there was a constitutional convention of Cabinet secrecy, but Dicey told us long ago that conventions were not enforced

9. *Attorney-General* v. *Jonathan Cape Ltd.* [1976] Q.B. 752. For a useful account of the background, see Hugo Young, *The Crossman Affair* (1976).

10. See Harvey Teff and Colin Munro, *Thalidomide: The Legal Aftermath* (1976).

by courts, and the judge (Lord Widgery C.J.) soon made it clear that he held by that view. The other string to the Attorney-General's bow was what the judge perhaps euphemistically described as the "developing" law of confidence.[11] It had already escaped from the workplace to the bedchamber. The question was whether it could make the further jump to Whitehall, or whether, as the defendants contended, that would be "another large and unjustified leap forward".[12] The Lord Chief Justice saw no ground for confining the law to private confidences and excluding public confidences, and so he held that the law would apply to Cabinet secrets, as the obligation of confidentiality in respect of them was generally understood. However, there was to be a possibly unexpected twist. Lord Widgery considered that the public interest had a more important role to play where government confidences were concerned. He said that the plaintiff must show not only a breach of confidence, but that "the public interest requires that the publication be restrained", and "that there are no other facets of the public interest contradictory to and more compelling than that relied on".[13] In the case before him, at an interval of 10 years from the events described, he was not persuaded that it was the duty of the court to restrain publication.

Lord Widgery's pragmatic judgment left several questions unanswered,[14] and left the boundaries of the law of confidence uncertain, but it was not appealed. Naturally, the defendants could not appeal, as they had won, although the extension of the law of confidence into the area of the business of government carried disturbing implications for authors and publishers.

However, the essentials of Lord Widgery's approach were followed in an Australian case a few years later, *Commonwealth of Australia* v. *John Fairfax & Sons Ltd.*[15] The case concerned

11. *Attorney-General* v. *Jonathan Cape Ltd.* [1976] Q.B. 752, 769.
12. *Ibid.* at p. 769.
13. *Ibid.* at p. 770.
14. One particular result was that a committee of privy councillors on ministerial memoirs was appointed, under the chairmanship of Viscount Radcliffe, to make recommendations for the future. The committee did not recommend the enactment of legislation, instead preferring a more formalised vetting system, compliance with which would rest on obligations of honour. The Report (Cmnd. 6386) was accepted by the government, and its recommendations were implemented.
15. (1980) 147 C.L.R. 39.

a book entitled *Documents on Australian Defence and Foreign Policy 1968–1975* consisting of government documents and cable messages, presumably leaked by a public servant in breach of his duty. The Australian government learned of the book late in the day, just before its publication date, and at a time when two newspapers were proceeding to the publication of extracts. It obtained *ex parte* injunctions as quickly as possible, but not before the distribution of some 100 advance copies of the book and the sale of some 60,000 copies of newspapers containing the first extracts.

In the High Court of Australia, Mason J. had to decide whether to grant interim injunctions against further publication. He did grant injunctions on the basis of a breach of the government's copyright in the material, rejecting the defence of fair dealing.

He would not, however, have granted the injunctions sought on the basis of a breach of confidence. Concerning the submissions on the law of confidence, he had this to say:

"The equitable principle has been fashioned to protect the personal, private and proprietary interests of the citizen, not to protect the very different interests of the executive government ... This is not to say that equity will not protect information in the hands of the government, but it is to say that when equity protects government information it will look at the matter through different spectacles...

It may be a sufficient detriment to the citizen that disclosure of information relating to his affairs will expose his actions to public discussions and criticism. But it can scarcely be a relevant detriment to the government that publication of material concerning its actions will merely expose it to public discussion and criticism. It is unacceptable in our democratic society that there should be a restraint on the publication of information relating to government when the only vice of that information is that it enables the public to discuss, review and criticize government action."[16]

The judge noted that the material in question did not include defence or military secrets, the publication of which would be harmful to national security. That being so, he did not consider that the degree of embarrassment which the government might suffer through disclosure was a sufficient reason to justify its prevention on a basis of breach of confidence. Besides, there was a second aspect which resolved the question: the secrets

16. *Ibid*. at pp. 51–52.

were out. The publication which had already taken place was such, he considered, that the information in the book would become known to an ever-widening group of persons.

SPYCATCHER AND THE LAW OF CONFIDENCE

Both the *Crossman Diaries* case and the Australian case involved governments trying to suppress disclosures, and so of course did the litigation aimed at preventing the publication of *Spycatcher* or its contents. Before we lose sight of the point, it is worth observing that there are two sides to the coin. As well as information about government, which governments may wish to suppress, the government has information about us, which we may wish to suppress. The state in its many manifestations amasses a huge amount of information from and about individuals, often compulsorily. Generally, there are statutory provisions which guard against the unauthorised disclosure of this information, but another shield is provided by the breach of confidence action, which would be available in circumstances like these.[17] So far, however, all the running has been made *by* governments.

The resolution of the *Spycatcher* affair is still comparatively fresh in our minds. After earlier interlocutory proceedings,[18] not to mention proceedings in various other states and territories presumed to be friendly,[19] the Attorney-General's application for permanent injunctions was heard by Scott J. at the end of 1987, and his appeals were heard by the Court of Appeal and

17. See Francis Gurry, *Breach of Confidence* (1984), Ch. 10.

18. *Attorney-General* v. *Observer Ltd.* (1986) 136 N.L.J. 799; *Attorney-General* v. *Guardian Newspapers Ltd.* [1987] 3 All E.R. 316.

19. In particular, in Australia, New Zealand and Hong Kong. For the proceedings in Australia, see *Attorney-General (U.K.)* v. *Heinemann Publishers Australia Pty. Ltd.* (1987) 8 N.S.W.L.R. 341 (New South Wales Supreme Court), (1987) 75 A.L.R. 353 (New South Wales Court of Appeal), (1988) 78 A.L.R. 449 (High Court of Australia). In New Zealand: *Attorney-General for England and Wales* v. *Wellington Newspapers Ltd.* [1988] 1 N.Z.L.R. 129. It was accepted, however, that any attempt to suppress publication in the United States would be futile, in view of the Supreme Court's decision in the Pentagon Papers case: *New York Times Co.* v. *United States* (1971) 403 U.S. 713.

the House of Lords in 1988.[20] The three courts were in substantial agreement. In summary, the House of Lords declined to grant injunctions against further newspaper coverage, or against further serialisation of the book by the *Sunday Times*, or in general terms such as would restrain similar publications in future. The reasoning was principally that the information in the book had entered the public domain, and so was no longer confidential. Some earlier reports in the *Guardian* and the *Observer* newspapers were held not to be in breach of the law, but an earlier extract in the *Sunday Times*, which Lord Keith of Kinkel described as having appeared as a result of "peculiarly sneaky methods",[21] was, and the newspaper was held liable to account for profits resulting from that one issue.

It is appropriate to review the principles of the law of confidence, as they apply to goverment information, in the light of the *Spycatcher* judgments, as well as the earlier cases.

The general principles of the law were clearly stated by Lord Goff:

"... a duty of confidence arises when confidential information comes to the knowledge of a person (the confidant) in circumstances where he has notice, or is held to have agreed, that the information is confidential, with the effect that it would be just in all the circumstances that he should be precluded from disclosing the information to others ... The existence of this broad general principle reflects the fact that there is such a public interest in the maintenance of confidences, that the law will provide remedies for their protection.

To this broad general principle, there are three limiting principles ... The first ... is that the principle of confidentiality only applies to information to the extent that it is confidential ...

The second limiting principle is that the duty of confidence applies neither to useless information, nor to trivia ...

The third limiting principle ... is that, although the basis of the law's protection of confidence is that there is a public interest that confidences should be preserved and protected by the law, nevertheless that public interest may be outweighed by some other countervailing public interest which favours disclosure ..."[22]

If we ask whether the principles generally applicable to the

20. *Attorney-General* v. *Guardian Newspapers Ltd. (No. 2)* [1988] 3 All E.R. 545; [1988] 2 W.L.R. 805 (Scott J. and C.A.), [1988] 3 W.L.R. 776 (H.L.).

21. [1988] 3 All E.R. 545, 644.

22. [1988] 3 All E.R. 545, 658–659

action apply when it is confidential information about government that is involved, the answer must be a qualified assent.

The major qualification is on a central point. The courts have founded the action for breach of confidence on a basis of public policy or, as they prefer to call it, the public interest. But whereas there is a public interest in the preservation of confidences which in private actions may be sufficient—there was some difference of opinion on the need for detriment to be shown in private actions[23]—what is clear is that, when information about the government is concerned, there are other public interests favouring disclosure. Therefore, the courts will not lend their assistance unless persuaded that *detriment to the national interest* would result from disclosure. It is an "additional requirement",[24] as Lord Goff put it. The government is treated differently, partly because it has no private life or personal feelings[25] to be hurt, but partly because, in a free society, "the workings of government should be open to scrutiny and criticism".[26] From this it might be inferred that freedom of speech, as required in English law by article 10 of the European Convention for the Protection of Human Rights and Fundamental Freedoms, is at least one of the public interests to be weighed in the balance. There was general support for that view,[27] although the Master of the Rolls was careful to stress that newspapers enjoyed no special status[28] and several of the judges emphasised that even where the public interest favoured a disclosure of confidential information, it did not follow that disclosure to or by the media was justified, for a more limited disclosure might be appropriate.[29]

23. In the House of Lords, Lord Griffiths considered that the element had to be established, Lord Keith thought otherwise, and Lord Goff left the question open: [1988] 3 All E.R. 545, 640, 650, 659.
24. [1988] 3 All E.R. 545, 660.
25. [1988] 3 All E.R. 545, 640 (*per* Lord Keith).
26. [1988] 3 All E.R. 545, 660 (*per* Lord Goff).
27. [1988] 3 All E.R. 545, for example at pp. 580–582 (*per* Scott J.), at p. 623 (*per* Bingham L.J.), at p. 640 (*per* Lord Keith), at p. 652 (*per* Lord Griffiths) and at p. 660 (*per* Lord Goff).
28. [1988] 3 All E.R. 545, 600.
29. [1988] 3 All E.R. 545, for example at p. 584 (*per* Scott J.), at p. 596 (*per* Sir John Donaldson M.R.), at p. 630 (*per* Bingham L.J.), at p. 649 (*per* Lord Griffiths) and at p. 659 (*per* Lord Goff). On this, see *Francome* v. *Mirror Group Newspapers Ltd.* [1984] 2 All E.R. 408.

This approach to government information, which puts the government in a special position as regards breach of confidence actions, is greatly to be welcomed. To treat the Crown as being rather different from a private litigant is appropriate, because it is realistic. The approach, foreshadowed in the *Crossman Diaries* case and the Australian case, has essentially been confirmed in the recent litigation.

However, there are perhaps one or two additional items on the debit side. In some respects, the courts have arguably been rather less stringent in their demands when government information has been involved. For example, when the parties are in a private relationship, it is the confider who has standing to enforce the obligation when a defendant has used confidential information "directly or indirectly obtained"[30] from him. In the *Crossman* and *Spycatcher* cases, the courts have been content to accept the Attorney-General as plaintiff on behalf of the Crown, although he cannot realistically be regarded as "the confider". No doubt, the courts' acceptance is understandable in view of the Attorney-General's role in respect of the Crown[31] as well as his position in the courts, but the fiction perhaps creates a rather dangerous precedent so far as the law of confidence is concerned.

If there is some doubt about whether the Attorney-General or, for that matter, the Crown, is really "the confider", a related point is even more troubling. That point is whether the information was actually transmitted to Mr Wright within a confidential relationship. Scott J. expressed the point most clearly:

"[The] duty has been described throughout the case as a duty of 'confidence' . . . But in cases like the present the description is, in my opinion, apt to be misleading. The duty contended for by the Crown would apply to information which had not been imparted to Mr Wright by anyone, but which he himself had unearthed by his own endeavours. There would be no 'confider' or 'confidant' in relation to information of that character. The duty would apply also to information which had been imparted to Mr Wright by someone to whom he owed no

30. *Saltman Engineering Co. Ltd.* v. *Campbell Engineering Co. Ltd.* (1948) 65 R.P.C. 203, 213 (*per* Lord Greene M.R.).

31. The status of the office of Attorney-General may have been further damaged by variant public statements as to the capacity in which he has been acting in these cases: see James Michael, "The Wright Case—The Attorney General's Role" (1986) 136 N.L.J. 1199.

duty of confidence at all. The duty contended for would, prima facie, apply to all information acquired by Mr Wright in his capacity as a member of MI5. The duty is more a duty of secrecy than a duty of confidence."[32]

Exactly so. Nevertheless, all the courts went on to dispose of the case by the law of confidence. In doing so, they have connived in some damage to its general principles. The well-established rule that the "information must have been imparted in circumstances importing an obligation of confidence"[33] seems to be suffering from a form of slippage, which renders the law uncertain and threatens to encroach further and dangerously on the freedom of the press.

CONFIDENCE AND SECRECY

Scott J.'s perception goes to the heart of the matter. In the *Crossman Diaries* case and in the *Spycatcher* litigation, governments have been employing the law of confidence, but what they have been seeking to preserve and enforce is *secrecy*. Moreover, since in both instances the information concerned was obtained in the service of the Crown, it was officially secret information, which the law, in the form of the Official Secrets Acts 1911–1989, was in principle capable of protecting.

One is bound to ask why, on these occasions, the law of confidence was employed, without notable success, and the law of secrecy was not. There is perhaps a general answer to this question, as well as more particular reasons applicable to the two instances.

The more general explanation may be found in the nature and standing of the Official Secrets Acts.[34] The principal statute, the Official Secrets Act 1911, was introduced in Parliament as an emergency measure necessary to deal with the menace of foreign spies, and was sufficiently well received that it completed

32. [1988] 3 All E.R. 545, 571.

33. *Coco* v. *A.N. Clark (Engineers) Ltd.* [1969] R.P.C. 41 at p. 47 (*per* Megarry J.), cited with approval by Bingham L.J. and by Lord Griffiths: [1988] 3 All E.R. 545, 624, 648.

34. See generally David Williams, *Not in the Public Interest* (1965), and "Official Secrecy and the Courts" in P.R. Glazebrook (ed.), *Reshaping the Criminal Law* (1978); David Leigh, *The Frontiers of Secrecy* (1980).

all of its Commons stages in less than 40 minutes. The Minister, Coloney Seely, gave the assurance that: "The actual change in the law is slight, and it is perfectly true to say that none of His Majesty's loyal subjects run the least risk whatever of having their liberties infringed in any degree or particular."[35] In fact, section 2 of the Act[36] created a blanket offence covering *all* government information. Communication of such information to anyone other than someone authorised to receive it or someone "to whom it is in the interest of the State his duty to communicate it" was an offence, as was the willing receipt of such information by a person who knew or had reasonable grounds for believing that it was passed to him in contravention of the law. (That is merely a summary, for it has been calculated that the wording of the section created 2,324 ways of committing an offence.) Thus, the width of the offence was enormous. Its rigours were to some extent restrained in practice by the need for the Attorney-General's consent to prosecutions, and by the nebulous concept of authorisation, which seemed to allow Ministers and some senior civil servants to disclose what they chose to.

But, if you legislate in haste, you repent at leisure. Section 2 had fallen badly into disrepute. In 1971, when a diplomat's report on the Nigerian civil war had been published in the *Sunday Telegraph*, the defendants were all acquitted at the ensuing trial, and the judge, Caulfield J., who ordered that their costs be paid out of public funds, suggested that the section, having reached the age of 60, "should be pensioned off".[37] In the following year, the committee of inquiry under the chairmanship of Lord Franks said: "we found section 2 a mess."[38]

In 1984, there was widespread criticism of the sentence of six months' imprisonment passed on Miss Sarah Tisdall, a clerk who had leaked documents on the arrival of Cruise missiles to the *Guardian*. In 1985, when Mr Clive Ponting was prosecuted for passing information about the sinking of the Argentinian ship *General Belgrano* to a Member of Parliament, the

35. 29 H.C. Deb., col. 2257 (18 August 1911).
36. As amended by the Official Secrets Act 1920.
37. See Jonathan Aitken, *Officially Secret* (1971).
38. Departmental Committee on Section 2 of the Official Secrets Act 1911 (Cmnd. 5104), vol. 1, Report, para. 88.

jury acquitted him in spite of (or perhaps because of) a direction from McCowan J. that "the interest of the State should be equated with the policies and interests of the government of the day". Inconsistencies in prosecution policy became apparent when in the same period Granada Television was not prosecuted for broadcasting an interview with Peter Wright, and neither the former MI5 officer, Cathy Massiter, who revealed details of telephone-intercept practices nor Channel 4, which broadcast them, was prosecuted.

If section 2 was already discredited in the early 1970s, it was badly sullied by the 1980s. From the government's perspective, it had become dangerously unworkable: it was badly drafted, and unpredictable in its operation, especially as it involved jury trials. From every other perspective, it was absurdly wide, over-severe, unacceptably obscure, and inconsistently applied.

Thus, one may understand why the Attorney-General might view the use of section 2 of the Official Secrets Act with something less than enthusiasm. By contrast, the law of confidence may have seemed attractive, especially as the hazards of trial by jury would be avoided and the standard of proof to be met would be that of the civil law, and not that required for criminal prosecutions.

The Official Secrets Act could have been used, not only as the basis for a prosecution, but as the basis for seeking an injunction. A disinclination towards the employment of that course may have owed something to a perception of the courts' reluctance to allow the civil remedy to be used in order to prevent the commission of crimes, as well as the standing of the Official Secrets Act. However, properly understood, the law is merely that private individuals who lack any special interest should not be allowed recourse to the civil courts for the purpose of seeking injunctions to restrain potential offences.[39] The fact that the Attorney-General may come to the courts for that purpose has been said to be "beyond doubt",[40] and in the circumstances of the *Crossman* and *Spycatcher* cases the special interests of the Crown *were* involved, so that there is no need

39. The leading case is *Gouriet* v. *Union of Post Office Workers* [1978] A.C. 435.

40. *Ibid.* at p. 507 (*per* Lord Edmund-Davies).

to ask whether in such instances the exceptional reasons which usually justify his acting were present.[41]

The *Sunday Times* newspaper and the publishers of the *Crossman Diaries* expected that the Official Secrets Act would be used against them, and their legal advice was that proceedings either for an injunction or by way of prosecution were likely to succeed.[42] So the decision not to use the Act was a great mystery to the defendants. A prosecution of the literary executors, who included Mr Crossman's widow and Mr Michael Foot, then a Minister of the Crown, may have been an unappealing prospect. But apparently legal reasons were decisive, for the Attorney-General actually conceded that the defendants were not in breach of the Act.[43] Presumably his view was that Mr Crossman's death somehow broke the link between his receipt of official information and its protection by the law. It must be doubted whether that view is right. Surely the executors were persons who had made an unauthorised communication of official information "obtained in contravention of this Act", an offence under section 2(1)(a)? Surely all the defendants were persons who had received official information, knowing or having reasonable ground to believe that it was communicated in contravention of the Act, an offence under section 2(2)? At all events, the Attorney-General, in his attempt to enforce secrecy, relied on the law of confidence and lost, when he might have relied on the law of official secrecy and won.

The Peter Wright memoirs presented a different kind of problem. The embittered Mr Wright had retired to Tasmania. The publication of his book was going to take place in Australia

41. Arguably, the kinds of exceptional reasons which usually underlie such actions were also present. Moreover, further support may be drawn from the willingness of judges in the cases under discussion to contemplate restraining publications on grounds independent of the law of confidence. Thus in *Attorney-General* v. *Jonathan Cape Ltd.* [1976] Q.B. 752 at p. 768, Lord Widgery C.J. said that there was "universal agreement that publication affecting national security" could be restrained on the ground of public interest. The legal justification for this view is not clear, but in *Attorney-General* v. *Guardian Newspapers Ltd. (No. 2)*, Sir John Donaldson M.R. touched on the existence of such a special right, and Lord Griffiths was in principle prepared to grant an injunction in the interests of national security: [1988] 3 All E.R. 545 at pp. 595, 654.

42. See H. Young, *The Crossman Affair* (1976).

43. *Attorney-General* v. *Jonathan Cape Ltd.* [1976] Q.B. 752, 767.

first, and the United States and other countries thereafter. The government could not use the Official Secrets Act in these other jurisdictions, since it was not part of their law. But the law of confidence was part of the law of Australia, and it was presumably judged worthwhile to try to abort publication there.[44] Following that, it was a natural progression to rely on the law of confidence in New Zealand and Hong Kong and in the English courts, when some newspapers began referring to the Wright allegations and the *Sunday Times* purchased the serial rights in the United States.

Of course, the Official Secrets Act could not be used to prosecute Peter Wright, because he was not here, and he could not be extradited, as offences against the Act are not extraditable crimes. However, the Act might have been used against others. Following the publication of the book, it might have been used against the *Sunday Times* and anyone else intending to publish the book or extracts from it here, and others who had communicated information or allegations derived from Mr Wright. Equally, before the publication of the book, the Act might have been used against the journalist and writer on espionage, Chapman Pincher, who had conveyed the substance of the Wright allegations in his book published in 1981, *Their Trade is Treachery*, and against Granada TV, which had broadcast an extensive interview with Wright in 1984.

Why was the official secrecy law not employed in these instances? As regards the Pincher book and the television programme, according to Sir Robert Armstrong's evidence, the government felt inhibited from acting to restrain publication because its information concerning them had been acquired in confidence.[45] Even if Sir Robert is no longer being economical with the truth, the explanation does not seem very compelling.

44. Significantly, it was the Australian courts' perception that the law of confidence was being employed as a vehicle for the preservation of another government's secrets that was fatal to the action there: see *Attorney-General (U.K.)* v. *Heinemann Publishers Australia Pty. Ltd.* (1988) 78 A.L.R. 449. On similar grounds, a judge in the High Court of Ireland declined to grant an injunction to prevent publication of another book of memoirs, *One Girl's War: Attorney-General for England and Wales* v. *Brandon Book Publishers Ltd.* [1989] F.S.R. 37.

45. *Attorney-General* v. *Guardian Newspapers Ltd. (No. 2)* [1988] 3 All E.R. 545, 558–563.

In any event, there would have been no such inhibitions as regards the later matters. No doubt, there is a preference for prosecuting the primary offender, which in the *Wright* case was impossible. For example, in the *Tisdall* and *Ponting* cases, the individuals responsible were prosecuted, while the recipients, the *Guardian* and Mr Tam Dalyell, M.P., were not. But that can only be a partial explanation. The general disfavour for section 2 must have been a strong factor. The government would also have found it embarrassing to employ the criminal law against publishers in this country, when the information which they were publishing, or hoping to publish, was information which could be published with impunity in other countries and was being published in many, and was information about events alleged to have happened here.

REFORM OF THE SECRECY LAW

The fact that section 2 of the Official Secrets Act 1911 had become more or less unworkable was no doubt one of the reasons which prompted the government to address the question of its reform. There was a White Paper[46] outlining proposals in June 1988, and then the government's Official Secrets Bill[47] was published in November. It later became law as the Official Secrets Act 1989.

There had been several earlier attempts to replace or modify section 2, following the publication of the Franks Committee's Report.[48] A Conservative government under Mrs Thatcher first attempted reform in 1979. However, the Bill it produced was unpopular, and its promotion also coincided with the unmasking of Sir Anthony Blunt as a traitor in a book written by Andrew Boyle. Members of Parliament discovered that Blunt's treachery had been known to some persons, but not to M.P.s generally, for the last 15 years, and the Bill which was before them merely

46. Cm. 408.

47. Printed as House of Commons Bill 9, 1988–89.

48. See Cm. 408, paras. 9–12; Norman Marsh, "Access to Government-Held Information in the United Kingdom", in Norman Marsh (ed.), *Public Access to Government-Held Information* (1987).

seemed apt to assist the preservation of such secrets, since it envisaged conclusive ministerial certificates as to the harmfulness of disclosures. The Bill had to be withdrawn.

More recently, a Conservative backbencher, Mr Richard Shepherd, had produced his own proposed reform. In January 1988, his Protection of Official Information Bill narrowly failed to achieve its second reading, when the government employed a three line whip to ensure its defeat, under an assurance that the Home Secretary's proposals for reform would shortly follow.

When Mr Hurd's proposals were announced in June, they were generally well-received, and in the Bill the government went further towards meeting such objections and criticisms as were made. The government did not feel that section 2 might be repealed without replacement, but it contemplated a much narrower role for the criminal law. Under the terms of the Act, as it became, six categories of official information merit protection. In summary, they are information, documents or articles:

- (a) relating to security or intelligence;
- (b) relating to defence;
- (c) relating to international relations;
- (d) obtained in confidence from another state or an international organisation;
- (e) the disclosure of which results in the commission of an offence, facilitates an escape from custody, or impedes the prevention or detection of crime or the apprehension or prosecution of offenders, or is likely to have any of these effects;
- (f) relating to or obtained from the interception of communications under warrants issued under the Interception of Communications Act 1985 or the Security Service Act 1989.[49]

Unauthorised disclosures of protected information may be criminal, but in most cases liability depends on a further test, of whether the disclosure is "damaging". Tests of damage, formulated in different ways, are stipulated for categories (b), (c), and (d) above, and a harmfulness criterion is inherent in (e). With regard to (a), a distinction has to be drawn. Members and former

49. A Security Service Bill was introduced almost simultaneously.

members of the security and intelligence services are to be liable for any disclosure. Others will be liable only if their disclosure is damaging, that is, if "it causes damage to the work of, or of any part of, the security and intelligence services ... [or is such as] would be likely to cause such damage or which falls within a class or description of information, documents or articles the unauthorised disclosure of which would be likely to have that effect".[50]

Despite criticism, the government rejected demands for the inclusion of "public interest" as a general defence, and also rejected a defence of "prior publication" as such. The Home Secretary claimed with some justification that the requirements of harm take account of these considerations to a reasonable degree.

How would the new Official Secrets law affect the kinds of case we have been considering?

A latter day *Crossman Diaries*, if it existed, could in principle be published without offending against the Official Secrets Act, because Cabinet secrets are not given any particular protection. It would be different, of course, if any information in any of the protected categories were included, for then there might be liability.

What about something like *Spycatcher Two*, being the further memoirs of Mr Wright or the memoirs of the British spy, A.N. Other?

If A.N. Other were in this country, then the threat or the reality of prosecution might well be sufficient to stop publication or further publication. The forecast flood of books following in Peter Wright's footsteps—for it is said that perhaps there are as many as 15 more in preparation—may not occur.

But the new law will not matter very much if Mr Wright or Mr Other has retired outside our jurisdiction. Their disclosures would be criminal, but they could not be prosecuted. It would be an offence for a British newspaper or publisher to publish the details here, if the prosecution could show to the satisfaction of a jury that the disclosure was damaging, as it is defined. That would probably be a sufficient threat to prevent first publication here, but arguably further damage will be

50. Section 1(4).

unlikely in cases where there has already been wide circulation abroad.[51]

The judgments in *Attorney-General* v. *Guardian Newspapers (No. 2)* possibly influenced the government's plans to some degree. The proposals in the June White Paper were modified in some important respects in the November Bill. In the White Paper, information received in confidence from other governments and international organisations was absolutely protected, but in the Act its disclosure is subject to a harm test. The harm test for the category of information relating to international relations was narrowed. The category of information useful to criminals was narrowed and made more precise. The category of information about interceptions, which became the only category lacking a harm test, was also narrowed and made more precise. Some of these amendments might simply be attributed to the Home Secretary's commendable willingness to listen to criticisms. But there were suggestions that the White Paper proposals were inconsistent with the tenor of judicial approaches in the litigation, where most of the judges had been troubled by the Attorney-General's contention that Crown servants owed an absolute duty of secrecy.[52] The modifications agreed should not only make the Act more widely acceptable, but should bring the law of official secrecy closer to the judicial perception of the appropriate limits of the law of confidence as applied to government information.

In fact, the other Bill which was published almost simultaneously, the Security Service Bill,[53] perhaps owed something

51. However, it is noteworthy that the test of damage is considerably widened by the clause which protects security or intelligence information "within a class or description ... the unauthorised disclosure of which would be likely [to damage the services]". The words are reminiscent of considerations sometimes advanced in cases on the discovery of documents.

52. An obvious difficulty in advancing this proposition in the context was that there were established defences to a breach of confidence action, including the defence that it was in the public interest that the confidential information should be disclosed: see *Lion Laboratories Ltd.* v. *Evans* [1985] Q.B. 526. Another difficulty in it was that, in Lord Brightman's words, "It is meaningless to talk of a continuing duty of confidence in relation to matters disclosed worldwide": *Attorney-General* v. *Guardian Newspapers Ltd. (No. 2)* [1988] 3 All E.R. 545 at p. 647 (and see Lord Goff's discussion at pp. 660–665). Of course, the root cause of these difficulties was reliance on the law of confidence (which does not envisage an absolute duty) rather than the law of secrecy.

53. It became the Security Service Act 1989.

to the *Spycatcher* affair as well. Peter Wright's allegations of bugging, burgling, bungling, and plots to destabilise a government, served to remind everyone of the very limited accountability of MI5. No doubt there are good reasons why the service should be put on a statutory footing, with its functions prescribed and its political neutrality ordained, and better channels of complaint and means of oversight provided.[54]

CONCLUSION

As there is a new and more workable Official Secrets Act, does it mean that governments will be content to rely on that, and will cease to enlist the law of confidence in their efforts to preserve secrecy? Unfortunately, it may not. In the White Paper, it was expressly envisaged "that there may . . . be circumstances in which it is right for the government to seek to enforce its rights on behalf of the public under the civil law of confidence, notwithstanding that no prosecution for a criminal offence is possible".[55] In fact, as we have seen, resort has been had to the law of confidence in recent years in circumstances where there could have been prosecutions. Even since the beginning of the *Spycatcher* affair, further resort has been had to it in attempts to restrain the broadcasting of the radio series, "My Country, Right or Wrong",[56] and to restrain the publication of a book by Anthony Cavendish, a former secret agent.[57]

It would be better, surely, if government secrecy were enforced, to the extent that it should be enforced, by secrecy laws. The law of confidence is not a functional equivalent, unless it is unduly stretched. Nor will the law of confidence generally

54. Change might in any event have been forced on the government as a result of complaints to the European Commission of Human Rights by Ms Patricia Hewitt and Ms Harriet Harman. Their complaints, under articles 8 and 13 of the Convention, were that the law provided no effective remedy for protection of their rights to privacy, rights allegedly infringed through surveillance by MI5. Their applications were found admissible in May 1988.

55. Cm. 408, para. 14. A disclosure by a Crown servant may also constitute a disciplinary offence, and it was also envisaged that the Civil Service Discipline Code will require amendment (paras. 71–73).

56. *The Times*, 4, 5 and 18 December 1987.

57. *The Times*, 2 and 16 January 1988, 9 March 1988, 25 April 1988.

provide a cure in cases where there has been or is to be publication abroad.[58] As Lord Keith noted with regret, "even the most sensitive defence secrets of this country may not expect protection in the courts even of friendly foreign countries".[59] The use of the law of confidence, which was backed up by big brother the law of contempt[60] in the *Spycatcher* affair, is still the subject of an application by the *Sunday Times* to the European Commission of Human Rights. It must be doubtful whether the restrictions imposed on the press and publishers in this country were "necessary in a democratic society" and were satisfactorily "prescribed by law", as required by article 10 of the European Convention for the Protection of Human Rights and Fundamental Freedoms. It may be that further legislation will be necessitated by a decision of the European Court of Human Rights, just as was the Contempt of Court Act 1981. Legislation on breach of confidence is in any event desirable so as to clarify the extent of the law and to confine it to appropriate circumstances.

In the *Spycatcher* affair, the use of the law of confidence was not only inappropriate and ultimately unsuccessful. It was also counter-productive, for it ensured that *Spycatcher* would be a best-selling book throughout the world. Besides, in a democracy such as ours, the making of undue efforts to preserve what governments have inappropriately categorised as "confidences", will merely have the effect of diminishing our confidence in government.

COLIN MUNRO

58. In fact, the law of contract and the law of copyright, when they are relevant, may be more amenable to enforcement. Cf. *Snepp* v. *United States* (1980) 444 U.S. 507.

59. *Attorney-General* v. *Guardian Newspapers Ltd. (No. 2)* [1988] 3 All E.R. 545, 646.

60. See *Attorney-General* v. *Newspaper Publishing plc* [1987] 3 All E.R. 276. Contempt proceedings against the publishers of the *Sunday Times* in respect of its publication of an extract, held to be in breach of confidence, were heard later in 1989.

CHAPTER 2

DISCLOSURE OF MEDICAL RECORDS: A CONFIDENCE TRICK?

In the nature of things, we visit doctors when we are not well. We may be at our most vulnerable, and confide information which we do not wish to be spread beyond the confines of the consulting room. Tensions are bound to arise when such confidences are not honoured. On the whole, doctors repay the trust placed upon them. However, it may happen that information obtained by a doctor in the course of treatment may raise issues of the wider public interest. In such circumstances obvious tensions arise as between the doctor's duty to the patient and to the community generally.

SOURCE OF PROFESSIONAL OBLIGATIONS

The primary source of the obligation of the physician is contained in the Hippocratic Oath. This states that "whatever in connection with my professional practice, or not in connection with it, I see or hear, in the life of men, which ought not to be spoken of abroad, I will not divulge as reckoning that all should be kept secret".[1] In addition, the International Code of Medical Ethics states that "a doctor owes to his patient complete loyalty ... a doctor shall preserve absolute secrecy on all he knows about his patient because of the confidence entrusted in him".[2] Finally, the Declaration of Geneva states simply "I will respect the secrets which are confided in me even after the

1. For text see J. K. Mason and R. A. McCall Smith, *Law and Medical Ethics* (2nd ed., Butterworths 1987), Appendix A.
2. *Ibid.*, Appendix C.

patient has died".[3] Note the absolute nature of these statements. They permit no exception on the face of it, and indeed certain continental countries such as France and Belgium have written into their criminal codes such absolute standards to be placed on doctors.

In comparison the British Medical Association[4] and the General Medical Council[5] would permit a number of exceptions which would allow information to be disclosed. The most obvious occasion is consent by the patient, however it is allowed that there may be occasions upon which it would be undesirable, on medical grounds, to seek the patient's consent. Although there are allowances that information can be used for accredited medical research purposes, ordinarily disclosure will only be permitted under specific statutory requirements, or in consequence of court orders. However, it is allowed that there may be an overriding duty to society to disclose, and as we shall see later, this is unquestionably a problematic area.

LEGAL REMEDIES FOR BREACH OF CONFIDENCE

According to the Hippocratic Oath, the consequences for transgressing breach of confidence are severe: "while I continue to keep this Oath unviolated, may it be granted to me to enjoy life and practice of the art, respected by all men at all times. But should I trespass and violate this Oath, may the reverse be my lot."[6] In the modern day setting, the doctor's ability to enjoy life and practice of the art following the breach of etiquette is governed by the General Medical Council. Under section 35 of the Medical Act 1983, they are empowered to produce advice to doctors on matters of ethics. In fulfilment of this power, they have imposed a strict duty on doctors to refrain from third party disclosure of any information learnt directly or indirectly in a professional capacity as a registered medical practitioner. Unless a doctor falls within one of the

3. *Ibid.*, Appendix B (as amended at Sydney 1968).
4. British Medical Association, *Handbook of Medical Ethics* (BMA 1986).
5. General Medical Council, *Advice on Standards of Professional Conduct and Medical Ethics* ("The Blue Book") (GMC 1985).
6. Mason and McCall Smith, *op. cit.* Appendix A.

exceptions considered above, then wrongful disclosure in breach of the obligation of confidentiality can lead to disciplinary action being taken against the doctor leading, in the extreme, to the doctor being struck off the medical register.

In addition the law may provide remedies for breach of confidence, most obviously in the form of an interlocutory injunction to restrain the breach of the obligation by the person in whom the confidence is placed. Thus for example in *Duchess of Argyll* v. *Duke of Argyll*,[7] which is considered elsewhere in this volume, the Duke was restrained from publishing marriage confidences in Sunday newspapers. The grounds of that injunction were that an actionable obligation of confidence need not arise out of an express undertaking but could be implied so that the courts would intervene to offer relief against the person in breach, and third parties in receipt of confidential information. There was no requirement, according to this case, for the source of the obligation to lie in contract or in a proprietary interest.

It should be noted however that public disclosure of information given by the plaintiff could release the defendant from the obligation of secrecy. The notion in this case that an obligation of confidence can arise out of particular relationships is endorsed by recent case law, in which *dicta* have pointed to the doctor/patient relationship as an example of the legal recognition accorded to particular professional confidences. Failure to observe an injunction will amount to a contempt of court and the imposition of legal penalties. It is however more problematic whether a patient can sue directly for damages arising from some form of breach of confidence. Such cases as there have been have arisen out of some breach of contract, or have been concerned with cases in which the information had an obvious commercial value.[8] For a patient within the NHS, the absence of any contractual nexus will leave the patient seeking some other form of common law remedy. In the law of tort, there is no direct remedy available, and there is a further problem of quantification of damages, where these amount to mental stress, resulting from unauthorised disclosure. The Law Commission have recommended that such damages ought to

7. [1965] 1 All E.R. 611.
8. See for example *Seager* v. *Copydex Ltd. (No. 2)* [1969] 2 All E.R. 718.

be recoverable where they follow unauthorised disclosure. This, they recommend, could be achieved by the creation of a statutory tort. However, this recommendation has yet to be followed. The case of *Kitson* v. *Playfair*[9] is often cited as an example of damages being awarded for a breach of the implied covenant of secrecy. The award of damages in that case, in 1896, was £12,000. However as Jacob[10] points out, this case should be confined to its rather peculiar facts, the claim against the doctor being based in the law of defamation and not breach of confidence.

It should be noted that although the law offers legal recognition of the duty of confidentiality[11] the doctor, unlike the lawyer, is not offered any formal professional privilege. Further consequences of this rule are considered below.

PATIENT'S CONSENT

It is clear that the positive consent of the patient as to the release of information discharges any duty of confidence placed upon the practitioner. Thus in *C.* v. *C.*[12] a request by both the petitioner, and the respondent to divorce proceedings, that the doctor disclose certain details of the respondent's venereal disease could not be resisted by the doctor on the basis that the release of the information would be a breach of the professional duty of confidence. Here the patient's consent was written, but a problem can be the extent to which consent may be implied. For example in teaching hospitals, the treatment of the patient, and disclosure of information about the patient often take place in the presence of others. The general view is that the disclosure to other practitioners, within the ambit of professional requirements, is in order. Presumably this is thought to apply to medical students, although any complaints concerning such procedures could be addressed to the Health Service Ombudsman.[13] Pro-

9. *The Times*, 28 March 1896.

10. J. Jacob, *Speller's Law Relating to Hospitals and Kindred Institutions* (6th ed., Lewis 1978).

11. See *Gillick* v. *West Norfolk and Wisbech A.H.A.* [1985] 3 All E.R. 402.

12. [1946] 1 All E.R. 562.

13. Under the National Health Service Act 1977.

fessional status is highly significant here for it is clear that the courts will restrain wider disclosure. In *Latham* v. *Stevens*[14] the courts intervened to restrain the use of a medical certificate for advertising purposes.

The extent to which the patient may be taken to have authorised disclosure to relatives is problematic. Some of these issues will be considered later. The outcome of the *Gillick*[15] case, by a narrow majority of three to two in the House of Lords, was that the advice of the DHSS was lawful in so far as it suggested that a child under the age of 16 could in certain circumstances validly consent to contraception or abortion treatment without parental knowledge or agreement. This sits uneasily with a GMC case in 1971[16] in which a Dr Browne was found not guilty of professional misconduct. Dr Browne had informed the parents of a girl who had already attained the age of 16 of her request for contraception. In the GMC's view, this action taken by the doctor was in the best interests of the female patient. It follows that in this area a young patient, not necessarily below the age of majority, cannot be guaranteed confidentiality in relation to family planning services. It is a matter of judgement for the doctor in question whether to inform the parents, and a doctor who can show that the judgement was exercised in the best interests of the patient taking into account the maturity and welfare of the patient in question, will not be found to have acted unethically by the GMC.

DUTY TO SOCIETY

In *Attorney-General* v. *Guardian Newspapers (No. 2)*[17] Lord Goff stated that the duty of confidence is accorded legal recognition, but went on to say that there was a limiting principle of great importance. This was that:

"although the basis of the law's protection of confidence is that there is a public interest which confidences should be preserved and protected by the law, nevertheless that public interest may be outweighed by

14. [1913] Macg. Cop. Cas. 83 (1911–16).
15. *Supra.*
16. *GMC* v. *Browne*, *The Times*, 6, 8 March, 1971.
17. [1988] 3 All E.R. 545 at p. 659.

some other countervailing public interest which favours disclosure. This limitation may apply ... to all types of confidential information. It is this limiting principle which may require a court to carry out a balancing operation, weighing the public interest in maintaining confidence against a countervailing public interest favouring disclosure."

It is important, however, to make a distinction between information which the public might be interested in, and information which is in the public interest. This is illustrated by the case of *X Health Authority* v. *Y*,[18] in which there was disclosure by employees of a health authority to national newspapers of the fact that two practising doctors were being treated at an identified hospital for AIDS. In this case, in the view of Rose J., the countervailing wider public interest was the freedom of the press, and the court accepted that there was some public interest in the material published. However, in the view of the court, such public interest was substantially outweighed when measured against the public interest in relation to confidentiality of AIDS-related information on patients' hospital records. This was not least because victims of the disease ought not to be deterred by fear of discovery from attending hospital for treatment.

This type of balancing operation is not unknown in relation to public interest immunity more generally. In the case of *D.* v. *NSPCC*,[19] the House of Lords upheld the right of the NSPCC not to reveal the name of a source of information in relation to alleged child abuse for purposes of a defamation action. In the view of the House of Lords, the wider public interest of persons volunteering information in relation to potential child abuse outweighed the rights of the plaintiff in the case to learn of the identity of the person making the allegations. Of late, the most detailed consideration of these types of issues has occurred in the case of *W.* v. *Edgell*[20] which, in the words of Sir Stephen Browne, raised "in an unusually stark form the question of the nature and quality of the duty of confidence owed to a patient". In this case the patient was detained in

18. [1988] 2 All E.R. 648.

19. [1978] A.C. 171. Query whether what is happening in these cases is the balancing of a private law right against a public interest of *W.* v. *Edgell*, *infra*.

20. [1990] 2 W.L.R. 471.

a secure hospital without limit of time following the killing of five people and the wounding of two others. Ten years later he had applied to a Mental Health Review Tribunal to be discharged or transferred. This application was supported by the responsible medical officer, but was opposed by the Secretary of State. The solicitors on the part of W. instructed Edgell, a consultant psychiatrist, with a view to preparing a report which could be used in support of the application. In fact the report strongly opposed the application, and expressed concerns at the patient's likely release or transfer. The consultant psychiatrist assumed that solicitors on the part of W. would place a report before a tribunal. This was never done, as the solicitors withdrew the application, but Edgell, on learning that a report had not been disclosed contacted the medical director of the hospital and eventually forwarded to them a copy of the report in order that W.'s further treatment could be assessed. The hospital then forwarded a copy to the Secretary of State who in turn sent it on to the Tribunal. On discovering the disclosure of the report W. issued a writ against Edgell seeking an injunction restraining the use of the report and damages for breach of confidence.

Scott J. refused this application holding that the duty of confidentiality to the patient was subordinate to the public duty to allow the proper assessment of W.'s mental condition. On appeal, the Court of Appeal stated that there were two competing public interests: that a mental patient should be free to seek advice and assistance from an independent doctor to whom the patient should feel free to speak without reservation, and the concern, in this case, for the safety of the public. It was the judgment of the court that, as between these competing interests, the balance came down in favour of the disclosure of the report given the "number and nature of the killings" and the need to provide those responsible for W.'s treatment and management with "the fullest relevant information concerning his condition."

In one sense this decision is a relatively easy one for the courts. Given W.'s past medical history, and the public law forum of the tribunal hearing, together with the obvious public interest concerning the possible release of this patient, it is easier to think of more problematic cases than this one. This is not to say that the case presented no difficulties. The procedure laid down under the Mental Health Act 1983 gave the authorities no right to know the substance of the interview between doctor and patient. It was therefore a mere matter of choice whether the doctor might disclose his report. However, in many parallel situations there may have been issues of professional legal privilege which might have been invoked to restrict disclosure of the report. It must be troublesome that the impact of the case is to potentially limit the rights available to particular sorts of patient in their dealings with their medical advisers.

On the other hand, in the nature of things, elements of public interest will not relate to every medical disorder, as is shown by the cases discussed below. Moreover, although the statutory procedures put in place affect the process of disclosure, and raise problematic issues, the fact of these procedures is an indication of the public interest involved. It is suggested that a more problematic case might be that in which a psychiatrist in the course of an interview reaches the conclusion that the patient is a danger to the public, even though that patient has no past history of violence. In the *Edgell* case, great weight was placed upon the GMC "Blue Book"[21] and the exceptions contained therein. In particular much consideration was given to the rule 81(g) which states that "rarely disclosure may be justified on the ground that it is in the public interest which, in certain circumstances such as, for example, investigation by the police of a grave or serious crime, might override the doctor's duty to maintain his patient's confidence". Great emphasis was placed upon this provision at both stages of the *Edgell* case, notwithstanding that the rules have no statutory authority as such.

In other instances the line seems to have been taken by the lawyers for defence societies, when asked for advice, that doctors should seek to pursuade patients who, for example, are subject to fits but who drive for a living, to refer the matter to their employers.[22] If, however, it becomes apparent that this has not been done, then it is generally suggested that the doctor contacts the responsible medical practitioner of the employer where possible.

21. *Op. cit.*, see fn. 5, *supra*.
22. For examples see the Medical Defence Union, *Annual Report* (MDU 1974).

As is seen above the lack of any protection available to the doctor akin to legal privilege exposes the doctor to the risk of contempt wherever the court makes an order for disclosure which the doctor refuses to meet. Nonetheless there may be occasions when the doctor feels some duty is still owed to the patient notwithstanding a request by the authorities for information. There are occasions when the doctor may decide to disclose on the ground, considered above, of overriding public interest, and not merely because the court has ordered disclosure. An example of this may be where the doctor agrees to provide information required by the court in relation to drug trafficking offences. In general, however, the doctor will seek the patient's consent to disclose the information required by the court, and in the absence of this will generally await a witness summons prior to volunteering the information. It is not impossible however that, notwithstanding the formal processes of the court, a doctor may decide that professional and moral duties outweigh any legal interest. A case in which this was classically true was that of *Hunter* v. *Mann*[23]—in this case a doctor was asked by a patient to pay a visit to the patient's girlfriend who had been in a car accident. The doctor advised both patients to inform the police, but did not raise the matter of whether he might disclose their identity if approached. He did later receive a visit from the police in connection with a stolen car which had been involved in an accident in which both driver and passenger had run away. The doctor refused to release information about his patients on the basis that this would be a breach of professional confidence.

Section 168(2)(b) of the Road Traffic Act 1972 stated that "any ... person ... shall if required ... give any information which it is in his power to give and may lead to the identification of the driver". The doctor was successfully prosecuted in the Magistrates Court under this section and fined £5. He appealed against the conviction, on the basis that the words "any other person could not have been intended to apply to a doctor bound by a duty of confidence to the patient". Moreover he argued

23. [1974] 1 Q.B. 767.

that the words "in his power" did not apply in this case, because he had no legal power to disclose this confidential information. This appeal was dismissed by the Divisional Court on the basis that the doctor was not being asked to disclose any confidential information but merely information which might lead to an identification. The case is interesting in so much as it dealt with the issue as a mere matter of statutory interpretation. The wider questions of the doctor's ethical duty were hardly raised, with the court treating the word "power" to mean little more than actual capacity and state of knowledge, and side-stepping major issues as to the limits of the professional relationship. It is interesting to note that, even following court proceedings, Doctor Hunter did not disclose the information which the police sought.

DISCLOSURE OF MEDICAL RECORDS

In addition to other forms of court order, access to medical records is of course vital to any successful medical litigation. Essentially disclosure is available under two sections of the Supreme Court Act 1981, ss. 33 and 35. Section 33 enables a person likely to be a party to subsequent High Court proceedings to seek an order of the High Court, against a person also likely to be a party to the proceedings, for disclosure of relevant documents before proceedings are commenced. Section 34 of the 1981 Act enables a party to High Court proceedings to seek an order for the production of documents, as in the case of section 33, but against a third party also, and after proceedings have commenced. Section 35 states that the High Court will lack the jurisdiction to make an order, if it can be shown that the order, if made, would be likely to be injurious to the public interest. The power to make orders under ss. 33 and 34 is in any case discretionary. Orders for discovery in accordance with these actions is governed by RSC, O. 27, r7A, which governs both discovery prior to writ and discovery against third parties once proceedings have commenced.

Prior to the introduction of these procedures in 1971,[24] it was impossible to compel production of medical records in advance of trial. The difficulties were obvious. Medical experts

24. By virtue of the Administration of Justice Act 1970, ss. 31 and 32.

had to attend trial more often, adjournments to study evidence were common, and out of court settlements were clearly deterred. In general, however, the health authorities and medical defence societies would disclose voluntarily if approached by a solicitor showing good *prima facie* reason. However, many of the possibilities now brought about by section 33, were condemned by health authorities as "fishing expeditions" and medical records would not be forthcoming.

Even after 1971, in a long line of decisions to the precursors to sections 33 and 34[25] health authorities tried to restrict disclosure to medical advisers only on the basis that wider disclosure might lead to the applicant discovering medical opinions, knowledge of which might be considered harmful if disclosed to the plaintiff. In these cases, *Dunning* v. *United Liverpool Hospital's Board of Governors*[26]; *Davidson* v. *Lloyd Aircraft Services Ltd.*[27] and *Deistung* v. *South Western Metropolitan Hospital Board*,[28] it was held that disclosure should be restricted by the court order to the applicant's medical advisers only and that such medical advisers should act as intermediaries between the authorities and the applicant and any legal advisers. In *McIvor* v. *Southern Health and Social Services Board*[29] the House of Lords had little hesitation in finding the words of the sections so plain as to provide no basis for the rule of disclosure to the medical adviser only. In addition Lord Diplock did not feel that the arguments against disclosure other than to a medically qualified person were "of general applicability or convincing". Lord Diplock was confident that legal advisers would take precautions to prevent information becoming known to the client and that "an issue arising out of the claim in the action" need only be disclosed so that "any relevant parts of the document can be covered up".

This in many ways remained unsatisfactory, because under the language of the Administration of Justice Act 1970, disclosure was supposed to be to "the applicant", a problem which the House of Lords had still not fully addressed. Moreover,

25. *Ibid.*
26. [1973] 1 W.L.R. 586.
27. [1974] 1 W.L.R. 1042.
28. [1975] 1 W.L.R. 213.
29. [1978] 1 W.L.R. 757.

the notion of Lord Diplock that in some ways the medical records could be edited posed the difficulty that the legal advisers would have to fully trust the producers of the document that the editing had been made in accordance with Lord Diplock's rule that irrelevant parts of the document could be "covered up". Sections 33(2) and 34(2) of the 1981 Act effectively clarify the decision in *McIvor* by providing as follows:

(1) that the court may attach conditions to the order; and
(2) that production should be:
  (a) to the applicant's legal advisers; or
  (b) to the applicant's legal advisers and medical or other professional advisers; or
  (c) if the applicant has no legal advisers to medical or professional advisers alone.

Either way, once a plaintiff or a potential plaintiff has appointed a legal adviser, then they should be able to see the report. "Legal adviser" is not defined but is taken in general to mean disclosure to solicitors or barristers.

Disclosure is permitted to other professional advisers, but this term is not defined. In *Davies* v. *Eli Lilly*[30] the Court of Appeal were happy to accept a disclosure to a scientific co-ordinator in a complex case (in this case *Opren* litigation) so long as the court were prepared to accept that the person concerned would honour obligations of confidentiality and agree that information be not misused. It is also important to remember that the above rules deal with disclosure by court order. It may be possible to gain voluntary disclosure in any case.

In general most of the problems will arise in relation to the section 33 procedure for disclosure in advance of proceedings. This will depend upon there being a *prima facie* reason for disclosure, and in *Dunning* v. *United Liverpool Hospitals*[31] James L.J. laid down the criteria as follows:

> "In order to take advantage of the section, the applicant for relief must disclose the nature of the claim he intends to make and show not only the intention of making it but also that there is a reasonable basis for making it. Ill-founded, irresponsible and speculative alle-

30. [1987] 1 W.L.R. 428.
31. *Supra*, fn. 26 at p. 593.

gations or allegations based merely on hope would not provide a reasonable basis for an intended claim in subsequent proceedings."

Whilst this is so, it must be borne in mind, in seeking disclosure, that there will be some instances in which it is clear that injury has befallen a patient, but beyond that little is known as to whether or not this resulted from a breach of the duty of care. In such situations it may be possible to rely upon the *res ipsa loquitur*[32] rule.

ACCESS TO MEDICAL REPORTS

On 1 January 1989 the Access to Medical Reports Act 1988 came into force. The Act is intended to establish a right of access to reports provided by medical practitioners for employment or insurance purposes. In relation to employment, this will cover situations in which an employer or a former employer requires a medical report about an employee. The Act also extends to medical reports sought by a potential employer. The insurance provisions are similar. It is becoming less common for insurance companies to seek medical reports as a prior condition even for life insurance. Often sufficient information can be gleaned from questions relating to age, medical history and social habits—smoking being the obvious example. The spread of AIDS has made this type of questioning more likely. However, if the insurance company does require a report the Act will give the patients the right of access to it. This is equally true of other reports required by insurance companies, so that a report required to verify an insurance claim is covered.

The rights under the Act apply at various stages in the process of obtaining the report. They can be summarised as follows:

(1) Before the application for a report: the subject of the report has the right to be notified of the application and to withhold consent to it. The person seeking the report must inform subjects of their rights under the Act.
(2) Before the report is supplied: when the subjects have given their consent, they may demand the right to see

32. See *Saunders* v. *Leeds Western Health Authority and Robinson* (1985) 82 L.S. Gaz. 1491.

the report before it is supplied. The person seeking the report will have to tell the medical practitioners this, and the practitioner will be required to allow access to the subjects.

(3) After access to the report is gained: the report cannot be supplied unless the subjects have notified the medical practitioner of their consent. They are entitled before giving consent to ask for amendments to be made if the report is inaccurate or misleading. If the practitioner is not prepared to amend the report, they are permitted to attach a statement outlining their disagreement.

Prior to the Act, disclosure of a medical report directly to an employer or insurance company may well have been considered a breach of professional confidence on the part of the doctor. Nonetheless the Act is welcome in clarifying the position and laying down procedures, although there remains certain elements which are less than satisfactory.

There are exemptions. The report, or parts of it, need not be disclosed if it might reveal information about another person (other than a health professional). This seems an appropriate safeguard. However the doctor need not disclose if, as a matter of clinical judgement, the disclosure would be likely to cause serious harm to the physical or mental health of the individual or would indicate the intentions of the doctor in relation to the individual.[33] The latter will not please those who view medical paternalism as already too wide and patient autonomy too narrow, but there may be exceptional situations involving serious mental illness which may justify the exemption.

A medical report is defined as a report prepared by a medical practitioner responsible for the clinical care of the patient.[34] However employers or insurance companies could choose to use their company doctor to draft the medical report. Since that doctor is unlikely to be responsible for your clinical care, a subject would have no right of access to it. Also the Act implicitly assumes all reports are written, and although an oral report

33. These exemptions mirror those under the Data Protection (Subject Access Modification) (Health) Order 1987 which is considered below—see also the comments thereto.

34. Section 2(1).

might fall within the language of the statute, it may be difficult to adapt the procedures to suit.

The Act provides the right to apply to the County Court to ensure compliance with the procedures. It does not provide any mechanism for compensation if the procedures are breached to a person's detriment. Finally, it is unfortunate that the Act is limited to employment and insurance purposes. Medical reports are sought in many other contexts—social security, housing, vehicle licensing—in which an inaccurate report is no less unfortunate. Nonetheless the Act is welcome in promoting the vigilance of both companies and doctors in handling sensitive information.

DATA PROTECTION

The Data Protection Act 1984 is aimed at the prevention of holding inaccurate information in computerised records and at disclosing the existence of such computerised records where they exist. It offers a right to see the records and ensure their accuracy. Note that, although the Act only applies to computerised records, it does provide a back door route to records for those practices and authorities who have computerised medical files. Under section 29(1) of the Act, the Secretary of State is empowered to exempt certain categories of data, one of which is personal data concerning physical or mental health of the data subject. The power is one of either granting total exemption or modifying the operation of the access provisions. In general this is subject to the Secretary of State being satisfied that, given the nature of the information, confidentiality ought to prevent the availability of subject access. From an early stage in the life of the Act it was made known that these powers would be used to restrict the disclosure of certain personal health data. This has been done in the form of the Data Protection (Subject Access Modification) (Health) Order 1987.[35] Under this statutory instrument, permission is given to withhold data which might otherwise have to be disclosed in line with the current Act. In consequence it is possible to refuse to disclose personal data on the physical and/or mental health of the data subject

35. S.I. 1987 No. 1903.

which is held by a health professional. This exemption also applies to any other person, provided that the information constituting the data was first recorded by, or on behalf of, a health professional. On this basis the exemption could extend to an employer or insurance company holding medical reports on a computerised file.

However, it must be noted that the withholding of information under this order is permissible only on two grounds.[36] These are that the data will be likely to:

(1) cause serious harm to the physical or mental health of the data subject; or
(2) lead the data subject to identify another person (other than a health professional who has been involved in the care of the data subject) who has not consented to the disclosure of his or her identity.

This latter ground, which does not apply to health professionals involved in the care of the particular patient, will presumably mean that a data subject cannot, by searching his or her own health records, discover information relating to the health records of any other person. Note that both grounds involve an element of judgement (e.g. as to whether serious harm is likely to result). In each the decision on disclosure is that of the health professional, a non-health professional being required under the order to consult the medical practitioner responsible for the clinical data ("an appropriate health professional") before deciding whether or not to supply the health data required. It was the hope of the Data Protection Registrar, at the time of the order, that withholding disclosure on the grounds of serious physical or mental harm would be rarely used.[37] It is not absolutely impossible that certain rare data subjects could suffer some harm to their mental health by the disclosure of health records. It is much less easy to see that there will be many occasions in which the doctor could decide that the physical health of the data subject will suffer "serious harm" as the result of the disclosure of information about himself or herself.

36. *Ibid.* reg. 2(a) and (b).
37. Circular from the office of the Data Protection Registrar, November 1987.

Note in the absence of any ability to obtain disclosure by one of the above methods, there is no immediate access to medical records. This is because ownership of the records is generally held by the doctor or the hospital in question. Clearly the physical form of the records in terms of the files themselves belongs to the medical practitioner in question, and it is difficult for the patient to exert any intellectual property rights in the content.[38] There is comparatively little case law on the issue of the patients' rights in their own medical notes, but in the Scottish case of *Boyle* v. *Glasgow Royal Infirmary and Associated Hospitals*[39] it was said that the documents kept by a hospital are for their own purposes to assist their staff in the care and treatment of the patient. Whilst the patient may have an interest in the contents of the documents, this does not mean that the document belongs to the patient in question. To quote Lord Cameron:

> "the record of a patient's condition and treatment are not kept for the purposes of being made available to the patient on call, but so that a full and complete record of that patient's condition treatment and response or reaction to treatment may be kept. They may be valuable as adjunct to research and the advancement of medical science, they may be valuable for further treatment of the patient in other or recurring circumstances and it is obvious that those who make or keep them must be wholly free to state fully and frankly what they have to note, express or record."[40]

AIDS-RELATED INFORMATION

Even though the law seems to give relatively limited rights to patients regarding information about themselves, that body of law nonetheless proceeds from the basis that information relating to health and health status generally is a private matter. However, in one field this is particularly true, as the regulations governing disclosure of information relating to communicable diseases tend to illustrate. The rationale is presumably that persons can be stigmatised by the fact that they are suffering from

38. Since *Boardman* v. *Phipps* [1966] 3 All E.R. 721 would seem to be authority for the proposition that a person imparting mere knowledge to another has no general basis upon which (s)he can retain rights in or control the use of that knowledge.

39. 1969 S.C. 72.

40. *Ibid.* at p. 82.

a communicable disease. Often this has to do with methods of contraction of that disease. In the case of AIDS, methods of contraction may include homosexual practices and intravenous drug usage[41] so that those suffering from AIDS may also be members of social groups who already suffer from various forms of stigma or engage in criminal activities. On the other hand, it seems relatively clear that the virus is unlikely to be spread by most forms of casual or everyday contact. Nonetheless we have seen that persons who are HIV positive are shunned in schools, hospitals and work places.[42]

In this context confidentiality has a clear public health purpose. Medical confidence will encourage persons to come forward for testing, education, counselling, examination and treatment. Indeed co-operation in relation to medical practices may depend on confidentiality. If it is to be made widely known that certain persons who have volunteered for blood transfusions have been rejected for unspecified reasons, then people may draw their own (perhaps wrong) conclusions. This may lead to persons refusing to volunteer blood or come forward for blood testing.

This problem has been identified for some time, as the practices in relation to venereal diseases show. The National Health Service (Venereal Diseases) Regulations 1974[43] confine the communication of information on this subject to medical practitioners alone and for the treatment and prevention of the diseases in question. However AIDS is not included within the 1974 regulations, notwithstanding the fact that it is primarily sexually transmitted. The AIDS (Control) Act 1987, on the other hand, requires a mass of statistical information, but to no stated or obvious purpose. Finally AIDS is not a notifiable disease under the Public Health (Control of Disease) Act 1984, but the Secretary of State does have the power to hospitalise, and if necessary detain persons under the Public Health (Infectious Diseases) Regulations 1988.[44]

41. See R. Green "The Transmission of AIDS" in H. Dalton, S. Burris *et al. AIDS and the Law* (Yale U.P. 1987).

42. *Newsweek*, 23 September 1985, p. 23.

43. S.I. 1974 No. 29, reg. 2, as amended by the Health Services Act 1980 (Consequential Amendments) Order 1982, S.I. 1982 No. 288.

44. S.I. 1988 No. 1546, reg. 5, modifying section 38 Public Health (Control of Disease) Act 1984.

Whilst the above provisions address the issue of whether physicians have a duty to report questions relating to the spread of AIDS, they do not resolve the problem which the physician may face in particular cases of whether there is a duty to warn sexual partners. In the case of *Tarasoff* v. *Regence of the University of California*[45] the court found in favour of a duty upon both psychiatrist and psychologist to notify Miss Tarasoff and her family of the likely threat to her life from a particular patient. Here the patient had expressed, during a counselling session, his intention to harm the plaintiff. Controversially the courts placed upon the holders of this otherwise confidential information a duty to disclose. There is some support for this view in earlier cases. In the case *Simonson* v. *Swenson*[46] there is *dicta* supporting disclosure of information given to a physician in confidence on the basis that it is received "subject to the qualifications that if the patient's disease is found to be of a dangerous and so highly contagious or infectious nature that it will be necessarily transmitted to others unless the danger of contagion is disclosed to them, then the physician should, in that event, if no other means of protection is possible, be privileged to make so much of a disclosure to such persons as is necessary to prevent the spread of the disease."

In the U.K. it is much more difficult to establish any leads into the question of whether a doctor would have a duty to warn a sexual partner of the possibility of contracting a sexually transmitted disease. In the case of *Bravery* v. *Bravery*[47] it was thought possible that a divorce on the grounds of cruelty ought to be allowed if a wife discovered that without her consultation or consent her husband had undergone a sterilisation operation. In fact in that case, as a matter of evidence, the wife could not establish her lack of consent. This might help establish at least that a husband had some responsibility to consult with his spouse before undergoing such an operation. It is certainly true that doctors in these situations would ordinarily counsel the patient to do so. However, there is a further step from this to suggest that *Bravery* could in any way be authority for the

45. 17 Cal. 3d 425; 551 P. 2d 334; 131 Cal. Rptr. 14 (1976).

46. (1920) 9 A.L.R. 1250, 1253; see also *Pennison* v. *Provident Life Insurance* Co., 154 So. (2d) 617 (La. 1963).

47. [1954] 1 W.L.R. 1169.

view that a doctor could inform the spouse of a patient of the patient's request for sterilisation. Moreover the difficulty in making out this case is compounded by the views of Denning L.J. (dissenting) in the case of *Bravery* to the effect that the performance of a sterilisation operation on man in the absence of some just cause or excuse is a criminal act *per se*. Albeit that this opinion is in dissent, it says a great deal about the change in social attitudes within this area over the last 35 years.

In the case of *Paton* v. *British Pregnancy Advisory Service Trustees*[48] it was said that the husband had no rights enforceable in law or in equity to prevent his wife from terminating her pregnancy by him, or to stop doctors carrying out an abortion which was lawful under the Abortion Act 1967. Given that this is so, there is no necessary duty placed on a doctor to inform the father of a child of his patient's wishes to terminate a pregnancy. However, none of these cases directly addressed the point whether a doctor could, in the protection of the health of the sexual partner of a patient, inform that partner of the risks of continued sexual activity, in the face of an absolute refusal by the patient to so inform.

The other area in which AIDS-related information creates difficulties of medical confidence is insurance.[49] The problem here, from the perspective of the life insurance company, is that younger males are usually a low premium group, but if HIV positive, will undergo prolonged illness which will prove fatal. On the other hand the risk to the insurance companies may be over emphasised, given that the persons most likely to become HIV positive are not likely to be strong purchasers of life insurance, being either homosexuals with a lack of dependants, or young drug users who have perhaps not given much thought to life insurance purchase. Insurance companies might counter that, given the long latency period of HIV, it is not always possible to look at the present lifestyle of an individual in order to assess that individual for insurance purposes.

Nonetheless one option for insurance companies in this area is to isolate a target population for whom life insurance is regu-

48. [1978] 2 All E.R. 987.
49. See R. P. Iuculano, "Life Insurance" in W. H. L. Dornette (Ed.) *AIDS and the Law* (Wiley 1987).

larly refused. This would include perhaps single males aged between 20 years and 50 years with no insurable interests and whose lifestyle might be indicated by such questions as residence, or leisure activity. The alternative is simply to use AIDS antibody testing. The problem here is that false positive results run at something like one in every 20,000 tests. The stigmatisation which may result from a false positive in addition to the difficulties that will then face that person in relation to obtaining insurance and employment are of sufficient concern that a number of the States legislatures have banned or restricted the use of blood tests in order to determine insurability.[50]

The insurance companies would argue for their part that the difficulty of false positives is matched by a problem which they also face of false negatives. Moreover they might argue that a process of triple testing can produce a degree of certainty to 999 cases out of 1,000.[51] They also argue that testing is preferable to the alternative of reducing the availability of insurance to a large male population. They also claim that there is little difference in principle between insurance applications which ask questions about smoking in relation to possible heart complaints, or to examine levels of cholesterol for similar purposes. However, this seems to pay little regard to the actual problems faced by persons who discover they are HIV positive. Perhaps the final problem, however, is that although insurance companies are experienced in handling information relating to the individual, the risks in relation to confidentiality of information in this area are, in terms of its social consequences, far more severe than much of the information that an insurance company would generally handle, so that there are well founded concerns regarding the guarantees an insurance company may be able to give in relation to such sensitive information.

CONCLUSION

The final section relating to AIDS crystallises many of the problems of medical confidentiality generally. Large issues may be

50. For a review of this see M. Scherzer, "Insurance" in Dalton, Burris *et al. op. cit.*; and Iuculano *op. cit.*
51. *New York Times*, 13 June 1986, A1.

at stake involving our every day lives and welfare and our personal well-being when medical confidences are breached. Looking to the law, however, we see two shortcomings. First there are few positive rights to discover information about ourselves kept in the form of health records. Where such rights exist they tend to be for specific and limited purposes and are not based on any wider notion that a person ought to know what is being said or discovered about them. Secondly there are few clear protections against the wrongful disclosure of the information, and even fewer remedies once disclosure has taken place. In general in relation to this area we depend upon the good sense and the ethical behaviour of the physician. That trust is generally repaid, but the outstanding question is whether, in terms of a formal guarantee, this is enough.

ROBERT LEE

CHAPTER 3

BANKING CONFIDENTIALITY

There is implied in the relationship of bank and customer a duty on the part of the bank to keep secret the affairs of its customers. This duty of confidentiality is a fundamental characteristic of the relationship, distinguishing it from other debtor–creditor relationships. It is a wide ranging duty, embracing all matters which touch upon the business between the bank and its customer. This will include entries on the customer's account and information supplied by the customer, however trivial: it is just as much part of the duty not to disclose a customer's name and address to the outside world, as it is to reveal details of some major dealings in which he is involved. The duty also covers information about the customer to which the customer is not a party such as inquiries which the bank have conducted relating to the account. Finally note that this duty survives the termination of the bank/customer relationship.

As the duty is contractual in nature, the remedy for breach is an action in damages.[1] However, it will be rare for the customer to be able to prove that material loss has been suffered as a result of the breach of the duty of confidentiality. Moreover, from the bank's point of view, the injury to their reputation resulting from indiscretion may outstrip the cost of an award in damages. Banks depend on public trust and confidence. Moreover the interest taken by the Banking Ombudsman[2] in complaints which are found on possible breaches of the duty of confidentiality acts as a potent deterrent. Even though it may

1. Though not punitive damages: *Guertin* v. *Royal Bank of Canada* (1983) 43 O.R. (2d.) 363.

2. For a review of the powers of the Banking Ombudsman see P.E. Morris, "The Banking Ombudsman" (1987), *Journal of Business Law* 131, 199.

be difficult in such cases for a customer to establish a loss, it is within the power of the Banking Ombudsman to suggest the bank makes reparation for the breach.

The duty consists of the requirement to take reasonable care of customer information. It is breached, therefore, where negligence leads to disclosure of otherwise confidential material. Although not hedged around with restrictions there are a number of accepted instances in which disclosure of information is permissible.

The statement of principle is to be found in the case of *Tournier* v. *National Provincial and Union Bank of England*,[3] which is the leading case on the duty of confidentiality.

Bankes L.J. said:

"At the present day I think it may be asserted with confidence that the duty (of secrecy) is a legal one arising out of contract in that the duty is not absolute but qualified. It is not possible to frame any exhaustive definitions of the duty. The most that can be done is to classify the qualification, and to indicate its limits ... on principle, I think that the qualifications can be classified under four heads:

(a) where disclosure is under compulsion of law;
(b) where there is a duty to the public to disclose;
(c) where the interest of the Bank requires disclosure;
(d) where the disclosure is made by the express or complied consent of customer."

It is perhaps easiest to examine these exceptions in reverse order. It is rather artificial to consider the circumstances in which a bank may have to make disclosure under compulsion of law, without first looking at those circumstances in which a bank may be under a public duty to divulge information.

DISCLOSURE WITH THE CONSENT OF THE CUSTOMER

If a customer gives his express consent to disclosure, then clearly that releases the bank from its duty of secrecy. Banks must take care to ensure that they only disclose as much as they are allowed to disclose by a customer and no more. The police often produce a letter signed by a customer authorising a bank to divulge details

3. [1924] 1 K.B. 461 at p. 473.

of its dealings with him. It is not uncommon for the police to argue that this type of authorisation empowers the bank to sign a written statement relating to the customer's account. However, it is difficult to interpret an authorisation to divulge details relating to an account as a general licence to volunteer statements relating to that account which might be used in evidence by the police against customers.

If a customer goes into bankruptcy or liquidation, then the trustee in bankruptcy or the liquidator stands in the shoes of the customer and can ask to have disclosed to him all details relating to the customer's account. The bank in such circumstances would not be acting in breach of the duty of confidentiality—it would be divulging information under the express authority of the customer.

The subject of implied consent is more difficult, and the Jack Report[4] recommended that this exception be restricted to disclosure with express consent alone.[5] In *Tournier* an example of implied consent given by Bankes L.J. was the "familiar case where the customer authorises a reference to his banker." In addition Atkin L. J. said that if disclosure were authorised in these circumstances it had to be on the basis of "an implied consent".

Obviously, it is very common for bankers to answer status enquiries raised by other bankers and it is a little difficult to see how the practice can be justified on the basis of implied consent, except where the customer knows of the practice and can be assumed to endorse it. Terms can be implied at common law where it is necessary to give business efficacy to the contract[6]: it is hard to see how it can be argued that it is essential to read such a term into a standard contract. It is difficult to see how disclosure to a commercial party requesting a reference gives efficacy to the bank/customer contract.

However, the practice is now so common and of such obvious benefit to the general business community that it seems almost inconceivable that, at common law, the courts would say that it is improper, being based on unlawful disclosures of customers'

4. *Banking Services: Law and Practice*, Cm. 622 (H.M.S.O. 1989) (hereinafter the Jack Report).
5. *Ibid.* paras. 5.33; 5.43.
6. See the judgment of Bowen L.J. in *The Moorcock* (1889) 14 P.D. 64.

affairs. Perhaps, if a case were ever fought on the subject the practice would be upheld as being in the general public's interest or as being in the interests of banks.

In recent times, a distinction has been drawn between so-called "white" and "black" information on customers' accounts. "White" information covers anodyne data about a customer—where he lives, what his dealings with the bank have been, what is the state of the overdraft. "Black" information is information about the creditworthiness of a customer where the banking relationship has gone sour.

The Banking Services White Paper[7] recommends a change in the *Tournier* rule in any future code of practice so that there can be no assumption of implied consent to the disclosure of "white" information to credit agencies.[8] Sharing of "black" information is considered in the following section.

DISCLOSURE WHERE THE INTEREST OF THE BANK REQUIRES DISCLOSURE

A bank's own interest can override the duty of confidentiality. Here, an example given by Bankes L.J.[9] was where a bank issues a writ claiming payment of an overdraft, stating on the face of it the amount of the overdraft. This is not a particularly useful example. A better one might be where the bank was threatened with a claim by some third party, and had to divulge some information about its customer's account in order to protect itself against a claim. Even here, it would be incorrect of the bank to divulge too much about the customer's account. It should only disclose so much as may be essential to safeguard its interest.

Referring to the problems of "white" and "black" information considered above, it has been argued that it is in order for banks to supply "black" information to credit reference agencies to which they subscribe. The basis for doing so would be that it would be in the interests of the bank—the pooling of information

7. *Banking Services: Law and Practice*, Cm. 1026 (H.M.S.O. 1990) (hereinafter the White Paper).
8. White Paper, para. 2.19.
9. *Tournier*, p. 473.

of such a nature is of clear benefit. However, there is less clear justification for treating "white" information in a similar way. The Banking Services White Paper[10] followed this line. It suggested that banks must be able to pass on "black" information to (e.g.) credit reference agencies. This was on the basis not only of the bank's interest but the wider public interest of encouraging responsible lending, and the consumer interest in not paying higher charges to bear the cost of bad debt. On the other hand, as is stated above, the disclosure of "white" information would require express consent. The White Paper suggests that these rules be incorporated in a code of practice supervised by the ombudsman.[11] However, such codes of practice are commonly used by the court in evidence as an indication of what good banking practice might dictate. It follows that the White Paper proposals could have dramatic impact in determining unresolved issues on the margins of confidentiality law.

WHERE THERE IS A DUTY TO THE PUBLIC TO DISCLOSE

In the view of Bankes L.J. there could exist "a higher duty than the primary duty, as where danger to the state or public duty may supersede the duty of the agent to his principal".[12] In extreme cases, there is no difficulty. For example, if it comes to the attention of a bank that its account is being used to prepare for the assassination of the Royal Family, then of course the bank is under a duty to disclose.[13] Suppose, however, that the police simply wish to trace a customer and the bank possesses information relating withdrawals from branches in certain geographical locations? Commonly the customer may be suspected of a financial crime. If the police visit the bank and ask for information, because they are investigating the customer in connection with a fraud, will the exception in *Tournier* mean that the bank ought to take what the police say at face value and

10. Para. 2.17.
11. At para. 2.21.
12. At p. 473.
13. Although this may be covered by principles of statutory disclosure, see the Prevention of Terrorism (Temporary Provisions) Act 1989 considered *infra*.

give all necessary assistance, including revealing details of a customer's account?

This problem was considered by Bankes L.J. in *Tournier*:

"A Police Officer goes to a Bank to make an enquiry about a customer of the Bank. He goes to the Bank, because he knows that the person about whom he wants information is a customer of the Bank's. The Police Officer is asked why he wants the information. He replies, because the customer is charged with a series of frauds. Is the Bank entitled to publish that information? Surely not. He acquired the information in his character of banker."[14]

It has been suggested that banks have to move with the times, and should be more robust in making disclosure when approached by the police. However, it is not for a bank to prejudge the guilt or innocence of its customers. There is an array of legal weapons which the police can employ to secure information relating to a customer's account.[15] However, if a bank suspects that it has information on file which may prevent the commission of future crime, then it ought to make disclosure.

It was suggested in the Jack Report that this exception no longer served a useful purpose.[16] Jack believed that statute law had already made major in-roads into customer confidentiality, and that statutory provisions alone should be regarded as the basis of a determination of when disclosure can be considered in the public interest. Once again the White Paper disagreed, stating that the statutory exceptions "affect only the very small number of customers who use the banking system for dishonest purposes".[17] It follows that disclosure in the public interest, as suggested by *Tournier*, remains unaffected.

DISCLOSURE UNDER COMPULSION OF LAW

As is indicated above, a bank does not act in breach of its duty of confidentiality if it is compelled by legal process to make disclosure. There are numerous statutes, probably more than the layman realises, under which the police and government bodies can secure disclosure of a customer's affairs from a bank.

14. At p. 474.
15. See Jack Report, Appendix Q, p. 408.
16. Para. 5.30.
17. Para. 26.

As a matter of common law, the court can also make various orders and issue writs requiring the bank to divulge information. These in-roads into confidentiality, listed in an Appendix to the Jack Report[18] were described in that Report as "seen by some as having Orwellian overtones".[19]

The aim of a great deal of the legislation in question is to provide the police with the means of gaining access to the confidential information held by banks, so as to assist in the general fight against crime. Banks are often placed in an invidious position, caught in the middle, between the police insisting upon disclosure and the customer insisting upon secrecy. Banks must preserve customer's confidentiality unless the police provide an order from the court or some other lawful authority which overrides their primary duty. Although banks need not look behind the orders or the authority to test whether it has been validly obtained, they should check carefully the ambit of the orders or authority, and ensure that any disclosure made does not exceed the limit imposed. What follows is a review of the major grounds upon which disclosure may be enforced.

THE POLICE AND CRIMINAL EVIDENCE ACT 1984

The general rule is that there is no requirement upon a bank to assist the police in investigating the affairs of the customer. This is particularly so where the police simply request the information because they now have the means to secure disclosure of confidential information relating to a customer even though that customer has neither been arrested nor charged.

Under section 9 of the Police and Criminal Evidence Act 1984, a police constable may make an application to the circuit court for access to special procedure material for the purposes of a criminal investigation. Special procedure material is defined in section 14 of the Act as any material in the possession of a person who acquired or created it in the course of any trade, business, profession or other occupation or for the purpose of any paid or unpaid office and holds it subject to an express

18. Appendix Q, p. 408.
19. Para. 5.08

or implied undertaking to hold it in confidence. The definition clearly embraces records held by a bank about a customer.

The procedure for making an application to obtain access to special procedure material is contained in Schedule 1 to the Act. A circuit judge can grant an order either requiring the bank to produce the material for a constable to take it away or to give the constable access to it, not later than the end of the period of seven days from the date of the order or the end of such longer period as the court may specify. Notice of the application must be served on the bank. There is no duty on the police to serve notice of the application on the customer.

This raises the question of whether or not a bank is under a duty to inform its customers of the application. There is nothing in the Act which indicates that a bank should do so, but it might be argued that a duty of this nature arises out of the duty of confidentiality. The better view is that there is no duty upon a bank to give any such warning. The duty of a bank to keep matters secret does not carry with it a duty to notify a customer of circumstances which may lead to the bank as a matter of law being compelled to disclose.

There is some authority for this proposition in the case of *R.* v. *Leicester Crown Court, ex parte Director of Public Prosecutions.*[20] In that case, the issue was whether under section 9 of the Police and Criminal Evidence Act 1984 notice should be given by the police to a person affected by confidential material, as well as to the body in whose possession was the material to which access was sought. It was not a case involving banks, but the comments of Watkins L.J. in the case are instructive. Watkins L.J. referred to the affidavit of the Crown prosecutor, which set out the considerations which gave the Crown anxiety in respect of circumstances where the holder of special procedure material might be subject to a threat and said:

"if a notice of application for the prevention of special procedure material must be served upon the suspected or accused person in related criminal proceedings, there may be circumstances in which the special procedure material to which access is required, may be held by person or corporate bodies who might be subjected to threats or susceptible to the influence of those accused or suspected persons."

20. [1987] 1 W.L.R. 1371.

He continued:

"It is desirable, in my view, that such consequences should be avoided. It seems almost inconceivable that Parliament enacting this part of the Act could have contemplated that a suspected person should be made aware of this essential part of the activities of the Police in making their investigation into criminal activity."

The case stresses the difficult position in which the bank might find itself, if it put the customer upon notice of a section 9 application. The customer might call for the mandate to be honoured and for materials to be passed over. The customer might then destroy these. The court make clear their dissatisfaction with this, pointing out that the only parties to a section 9 application are the police and the person in possession of the required material.

These points are all reinforced by the later case of *Barclays Bank* v. *Taylor*,[21] in which the customer, on being sued for a credit card debt, counterclaimed for general damages alleging that the bank had breached its implied contractual duty of confidentiality by not resisting a section 9 application. Not surprisingly, this counterclaim was rejected on the basis that the public interest in assisting the police outweighed any implied obligation which might otherwise arise. However, the Court of Appeal did indicate that this might be otherwise if "the bank knew something relevant to it which was not likely to be apparent on the face of the application or of the notice relating to it or might not be known to the police."[22] The question of whether the bank might inform the customer was left open: "there is nothing in Schedule 1 which forbids people like banks from telling their customers that such an investigation may take place. On the other hand there is nothing which authorises it either".[23]

However, some light is shed on this by another case involving Mr Taylor, the Divisional Court decision in the case of *R.* v. *Manchester Crown Court, ex parte Taylor*.[24] There, the applicant sought judicial review of orders made under section 9 of the Police and Criminal Evidence Act 1984 on the basis that the applications served on the banks did not contain all the

21. [1989] 3 All E.R. 563.
22. *Ibid.* at p. 569.
23. *Ibid.* at p. 579.
24. [1988] 2 All E.R. 769.

information required, which was instead communicated verbally by a police officer. Glidewell L.J. said, in dismissing the application, that the safeguards contained in the Act were safeguards for the protection of the person or body against whom the order was sought. The safeguards for the suspected person lay in the fact that it was for the circuit judge to be satisfied that it was right to make the access order. If this is so, it might be concluded that the passage of information by the bank to the customer is not an intended safeguard. On the other hand it is going rather far to say that because the Schedule does not authorise a bank communicating with its customer they cannot do so.

If an order is eventually made, the party affected by the disclosure has no *locus standi* to ask for judicial review of the order. When an order is made under the Act, the bank obviously must comply with that order. If the holder of material refuses to comply with a production order, the police will go directly to a circuit judge for a warrant, and the holder may be held in contempt.[25] However, the bank must be careful to comply only with the order as drawn, but no further. For example, if the order requires disclosure of all documents relating to the account of Mr A., it is not for the bank to interpret the order widely so as to assume that it extends to some vaguely connected account. In considering the duty of confidentiality, banks must construe orders literally.

THE BANKERS' BOOKS EVIDENCE ACT 1879

Bankes L.J. in his judgment in *Tournier* gave the operation of this Act as a classic example of disclosure under compulsion of law. A party to any proceedings, whether criminal or civil, can make an application under section 7 of the Act for the production of bankers' books. The expression "bankers' books" is defined in section 9 of the Act so as to include: "ledgers, day books, cash books, account books and other records used in the ordinary course of business of the bank, whether those records are in written form or kept on microfilm, magnetic tape or any other form of mechanical or electronic data retrievable mechanism".

25. Police and Criminal Evidence Act, Sched. 1, paras. 12–15.

The reference to "other records" is to be interpreted *ejusdem generis* and so, for example, the expression does not include paid cheques. If in criminal proceedings, wider disclosure is required it should be by way of an application under the Criminal Evidence Act 1984 or by the issue of a witness summons, requiring the production of listed documents. If in civil proceedings, wider disclosure is required, a *subpoena duces tecum* can be served. In criminal proceedings, the order can be made by a magistrate. In civil proceedings, the order can be made by application to the Master and is governed by rules of the Supreme Court Order 39, rule 13(2). It should be noted that proceedings must have been started before an order can be made—an order cannot be made, for example, where a crime is merely suspected. This was one of the reasons for the provisions in the Police and Criminal Evidence Act 1984 considered above.

In section 3 of the Act, copies of entries in bankers' books can be received as *prima facie* evidence of the existence of such entries and other matters, transactions and accounts recorded. The procedure will not be allowed to be used to secure disclosure of the bank accounts of third parties, who have no connection with the action. By the same token, the procedure must not be used as a fishing expedition. It is arguable that if a bank is not a party to the proceedings, it is only through use of the Bankers' Books Evidence Act 1879 that an order for disclosure can be made against a bank and that to issue a *subpoena duces tecum* would be inappropriate.

From what is written above, the following conclusions can be drawn relating to the banks' duties to assist the investigation of crime:

(1) if a crime is suspected, the police can obtain a Police and Criminal Evidence Act order under section 9 of the Act;
(2) if criminal proceedings have been initiated, the police can obtain a Bankers' Book Evidence Act order, but this is limited in its scope;
(3) if either order has been obtained, a bank can give a statement to the police merely acknowledging the existence of the documents and confirming what is said in them. However, if the statement is on Criminal

Justice Act notepaper, it should not be signed—lest it would be directly admissible in evidence against the customer at trial and it is not for a bank to volunteer such assistance;

(4) if a witness summons is issued, the bank, in its own interests, can sign a statement on Criminal Justice Act notepaper and release any documents referred to in the summons. The summons would be treated as sufficient compulsion of law.

DRUG TRAFFICKING OFFENCES ACT 1986

This is an important and difficult piece of legislation, under section 24 of which the bank may be guilty of a criminal offence where:

(1) it knows or suspects that its customer has trafficked in drugs;
(2) the bank holds on behalf of that customer the proceeds of drug trafficking;
(3) the bank has acted in such a manner as to facilitate the customer dealing with the proceeds of drug trafficking.

Conviction of an offence under this section on indictment carries with it a possible term not exceeding 14 years or a fine or both and on summary conviction imprisonment, not exceeding six months, or a fine or both.

However, the Act provides that where a person discloses to a constable a suspicion or belief that any funds or investments are derived from, or used in connection with, drug trafficking or any matter on which such a suspicion or belief is based, disclosure is not to be treated as a breach of the duty of confidentiality.[26] Further, a bank is not guilty of any offence in assisting a customer in dealing with the proceeds of the drug trafficking, if he makes disclosure before the dealing and the constable to

26. Section 24(3)(a).

whom disclosure is made agrees to the dealing or if the bank notifies the constable as soon as it is reasonable for them to do so after the dealing.

There are a variety of specific defences. If the bank does not know or suspect that the arrangement related to any person's proceeds of drug trafficking, there will be a defence. Likewise, there will be a defence if the bank thought that the arrangement did not facilitate a dealing in the proceeds of drug trafficking. The bank will also have a defence if it intended to disclose to a constable such a suspicion, belief or matter, but there is a reasonable excuse for its failure to do so.

A number of rules can be drawn from this:

(1) When a bank knows or suspects that it is holding the proceeds of drug trafficking, it should notify the National Drugs Intelligence Unit, this would not be unlawful disclosure. It would not be disclosure under compulsion of law, but the bank would be afforded a legal immunity. If the bank does not make disclosure in such circumstances, then it is of course running the risk of an offence.

(2) Every bank should have in place a system, whereby any possible dealing with drugs can be spotted. Of course, at the end of the day, it is for the bank to make a decision as to whether or not to notify the National Drugs Intelligence Unit. The bank must not intentionally act capriciously. If the bank reasonably suspects that the proceeds may be those of drug trafficking, it should disclose and it will be safe to do so. It is difficult to establish at what point a bank may be put upon notice of drug trafficking. If the bank gain knowledge of police suspicion of a customer, would this entitle them putting a stop on the account—or should they wait until arrest, or even conviction? Does any drug related offence indicate that monies in a customer account might be the proceeds of trafficking?

(3) It would be wrong for any bank to conduct the accounts of its customers on the mere say so of the police. This is especially true because the police can obtain restraint orders preventing a customer suspected of drug dealings

from using an account. Moreover the bank will be obliged to explain to any customer why an account has been frozen. Yet will the explanation that there is a problem under section 24 of the Drug Trafficking Offences Act constitute an offence under section 31 of the same Act? This latter section prohibits disclosure to a customer of an investigation under the Act where the bank has that knowledge.

(4) By and large, the bank must be governed by its own professional judgement. It is to be hoped that prosecutions under section 24 will be reserved for situations in which banks are put on obvious notice of the likelihood of drug trafficking yet make no inquiry into the movement of large deposits into certain accounts, allowing the withdrawal of funds without reference to the police.

THE CRIMINAL JUSTICE ACT 1987

The Criminal Justice Act 1987 gives wide powers of access to confidential information where serious fraud is being investigated. Section 2(2) of the Act provides that the Director of the Serious Fraud Office may, by notice in writing, require: "Any other person whom he has reason to believe has relevant information to attend before the Director at a specified time and place and answer questions or otherwise furnish information with respect to any matter relevant to the investigation..."

Section 2(3) provides that the Director may, by notice in writing, require that person: "to produce at a specified time and place any specified documents which appear to the Director to relate to any matter relevant to the investigation or any documents of a specified class which appear to him so to relate..."

The subsection goes on to provide that in such circumstances the Director may take copies or extracts from the documents which are produced and by section 2(3)(a)(ii) "require the person producing them to provide an explanation of any of them." These provisions could apply to a banker in an appropriate case and they could be used to oblige a banker to provide documents and statements.

At first sight some protection for a banker seems to be found in section 2(10) which provides that there shall be no requirement upon a banker to disclose information or produce documents in respect of which he owes a duty of confidentiality. However, section 2(10)(b) detracts more or less completely from the force of that provision by specifying that the banker can be required to disclose information and produce documents in the event that: "the Director authorises the making of the requirement or, if it is impracticable for him to act personally, a member of the Serious Fraud Office designated by him for the purposes of this subsection has done so . . ."

The powers of those investigating serious crime to obtain access to customer records kept by banks have come a long way from the Bankers' Books Evidence Act 1879 which requires the customer to be charged and a court order obtained; to the Police and Criminal Evidence Act 1984 which does not require a customer to be charged but does require a court order to be obtained; to the Criminal Justice Act 1987 which simply requires a signed notice from the relevant authority.

DISCLOSURE RELATING TO OTHER CRIMES

Much of the Criminal Justice Act 1987 is modelled upon the Drug Trafficking Offences Act 1986 in order to enable the court to confiscate the assets of offenders convicted of crimes other than drug trafficking where the benefit of the crime is at least £10,000. Section 98 of the Act allows that disclosure to the police by a bank of otherwise confidential information will not amount to a breach of any contractual duty of confidentiality where the banker has reason to suspect that the customer has obtained property in connection with an offence under the Act. It should be noted that in *Tournier* Bankes L.J. had stated that the disclosure of information to the police merely on the basis that the customer was suspected of a crime was unfounded.

In relation to terrorist offences, section 11 of the Prevention of Terrorism (Temporary Provisions) Act 1989 also mirrors section 24 of the Drug Trafficking Offences Act 1986. Here the target is terrorist funds. The same problems in relation to bank action under the 1986 Act are equally applicable here.

COURT ORDERS AT COMMON LAW

Although the above statutes by no means provide a comprehensive list of the statutory provisions relating to disclosure, they do cover the major problem areas which banks currently face.[27] In addition, there are a number of common law powers which must be considered. For example a *Mareva* injunction may support an order for discovery against a bank which is not a party to the proceedings. The classic example is where an injunction has been granted following a fraud and the court is anxious to trace the proceeds of the fraud. In such cases, the information held by the defendant's bank might be of assistance.

If granted, an order may be extremely wide—it does not have to be restricted in the same way as an Order under the Bankers' Books Evidence Act 1879 to certain categories of documents. In the leading case of *Bankers Trust* v. *Shapira*[28] the court granted: "an order which required disclosure *forthwith* of copies of correspondence, cheques, debit vouchers, transfer applications and internal memoranda".

A party obtaining such an order, sometimes called a "Shapiro Order", must undertake not to use the confidential information obtained other than in the proper course of proceedings. The bank affected is entitled from the plaintiff to a full indemnity as to its costs in complying with the terms of the order.

LETTERS OF REQUEST

Proceedings may take place in a foreign country which concern the affairs of the customer of a bank at one of its branches in England. The bank may be asked by the foreign court to supply information about the operations of its customer's account. The problem of conflict of law can arise since the bank has a duty of confidentiality to its customer under English law and yet it is the judicial authority of the foreign court which

27. For a comprehensive list see Jack Report, Appendix Q. In particular this paper does not cover revenue powers to seek disclosure under Income and Corporation Taxes Act 1970 and related taxation statutes.

28. [1980] 3 All E.R. 353.

is requesting the confidential information. Two methods can be used in order to obtain information. One is by means of letters of request[29], the other is by means of a *subpoena*.

The use of letters of request is regulated by the Hague Convention on the Taking of Evidence Abroad in Civil or Commercial Matters 1970, "the Hague Convention" which has been incorporated into domestic law by the Evidence (Proceedings and Other Jurisdictions) Act 1975, "the 1975 Act".

The procedure takes the form of a request by the foreign court to the High Court of England to order that evidence be furnished for the purposes of civil proceedings which have been instituted before the request in court. The evidence sought can simply be oral testimony of a witness or alternatively the production of copy documents. At first sight, this provision appears to be very wide. However, there are a number of limitations which have been imposed both by the 1975 Act itself and the court. In *Re Westinghouse Electric Corporation Uranium Contract*[30] the House of Lords had occasion to examine the whole question of letters of request in some detail and dealt with a number of the limitations.

It is clear from the provisions of the 1975 Act and from the *Westinghouse* case that the whole purpose of letters of request is to obtain evidence and not discovery. Where documents are to be examined the request must state specifically which individual documents are required and cannot rely on vague and general wording. Section 2(4) of the 1975 Act provides that an order shall not require a person "to state what documents relevant to the proceedings to which application for the order relates are or have been in his possession custody or power" or "to produce any documents other than particular documents specified in the orders". In the *Westinghouse* case the House of Lords emphasised this point. In that case it was held that wording such as "any memoranda, correspondence or other documents relevant thereto" would be entirely unacceptable.

Section 3(1) of the 1975 Act expressly provides that a person shall not be compelled to give any evidence which he could not be compelled to give: (a) in civil proceedings in the part

29. Also known as "letters rogatory".
30. [1978] A.C. 547.

of the United Kingdom in which the court that made the order exercises jurisdiction or (b) in civil proceedings in the country or territory in which the requesting court exercises jurisdiction.

Briefly, this means that if an order is sought against a bank it would not be obliged to reveal documents which were privileged either under the laws of the requesting court or under English law. In the *Westinghouse* case certain companies declined to disclose documents which may have shown that they were part of an illegal cartel and thereby rendered them liable to fines under EEC Law. The House of Lords held that they were entitled to rely on the privilege against self-incrimination and need not disclose those documents. A similar result would be obtained where, for example, the documents were covered by legal professional privilege having been prepared for the purposes of the litigation. Ellinger[31] suggests that this privilege exception extends to a bank's right and duty to maintain secrecy concerning its customers' affairs. He goes on to conclude that although it is true that a bank may be compelled at law to disclose information, he does not consider that this exception to the bank's right and duty to secrecy is wide enough to force disclosure where a foreign court has issued letters of request in repect of customers' accounts in this country.

It is submitted that Professor Ellinger is wrong on this point. He is confusing the question of privilege with that of confidentiality. If a document is suitably identified in a request and if the document is not privileged law or under the law of the requesting court, the bank can be and will be obliged to disclose the contents of the document.

Finally the *Westinghouse* case made it clear that although there was a duty on the courts to give effect to the Hague Convention as far as possible, in deciding to accede to any particular request they would give due weight to the national interest. In that case the Attorney General had intervened to make representations against a tendency of the United States courts to seek to exercise jurisdiction over foreigners in respect of acts done outside the jurisdiction of the U.S.A., with particular reference to the American Anti-Trust Law. It is clear that the House of Lords shared the Attorney General's concern and it is likely

31. E. P. Ellinger, *Modern Banking Law* (Clarendon Press, 1987).

that this will help to limit the circumstances in which a court will grant orders pursuant to letters of request.

Faced with the limitations of letters of request, the American courts have attempted to achieve their goal by ordering local officers of American international banks to disclose details concerning operations of overseas branches. Where the object is to produce documents then the *subpoena duces tecum* is served on the local officer. This places the bank and the officer in an extremely difficult position. If the officer refuses to obey the order he faces contempt of court proceedings in America. If he complies and supplies information or documents to the American court he may be liable to proceedings in his own country for breaching a duty of confidentiality imposed by the law of that country.

The American courts do of course take into, limited, consideration the prohibition imposed by the law of the country where the records are kept. However, there have been a number of decisions where the American courts have refused to allow a bank to justify its refusal to disclose documents by reason of the foreign secrecy law.

In *The United States* v. *The First National City Bank*[32], the U.S. Court of Appeal refused to allow a bank to justify its refusal to disclose documents by reason of German Bank Secrecy Law. It was held that the German law did not impose an absolute prohibition and further that the bank had not taken *bona fide* steps to seek permission to disclose. It would seem that if the bank had made a genuine but unsuccessful attempt to seek the permission of local authorities to comply with the American order or where it cannot be accused of seeking to use the foreign secrecy laws as a mere shield, an order for *subpoena* will be refused. In other cases they will be allowed causing considerable difficulties for the bank concerned.

English courts, in circumstances like these, will give considerable weight to the national interest rather than the policy of the United States. This tendency was of course shown in the *Westinghouse* case concerning letters rogatory. In another case, *X, A.G.* v. *A Bank*[33] a *subpoena* was served on the head office

32. (1968) 396 F. 2d 897 affd. 285 F. Supp. 845.
33. [1983] 2 All E.R. 464.

of an American bank for production in the United States of the records of a London branch of the bank concerning a certain group of companies engaged in the oil business. When the bank declared it intention to comply with the *subpoena*, the group succeeded in obtaining an injunction in the High Court restraining the bank from disclosing the records.

The fact that an injunction had been obtained in this country, restraining disclosure of the documents, would mean that the American courts would take a reasonable attitude and not penalise the bank for failing to comply with the *subpoena*. However, it is clearly unsatisfactory that a bank should be placed in a position where it risks being in contempt of court in whatever course of action it adopts.

CONCLUSION

It is vital to the bank/customer relationship that confidentiality is preserved. There are good commercial reasons why banks must be seen as the safeguards of both personal and, often, sensitive information about its customers and their dealings. In other financial arenas the drift of legislation, such as that on insider dealing, has been to prevent leakage of information: it says much for the banks that, in banking, the thrust of the legislation has been the opposite. A series of measures have sought to prise more information from the banks.

Often this has been for legitimate public purposes, but the statutes themselves have been less than clear. They have detracted from the simplicity and flexibility of the rules laid down in *Tournier* which have served so well. They leave the banks, in many instances, occupying the uncomfortable middle ground between authorities and customer. The code of practice which will follow the White Paper presents an opportunity to lay down positive guidelines in such instances. It would be helpful if this opportunity could be grasped.

MARK GILL

CHAPTER 4

BREACH OF CONFIDENCE AND PRIVACY

It has become increasingly evident over recent years that there has developed a growing disquiet with the activities of certain parts of the media and, in particular, the press. As the battle for increased circulation has intensified, there has been an increased willingness to publish sensational stories about well-known individuals from a number of different walks of life. On occasions, the people affected by these stories have been able to recover very substantial damages for libel[1]; the size of these jury awards perhaps reflecting public distaste at the intrusive and, to some, offensive behaviour of the press. What can be equally distressing, however, is a situation where the media publish true information about an individual's private life. In this sort of situation, of course, no action for libel is possible. The question which then arises is whether the law affords any redress for a person who has suffered an invasion of privacy.

It is possible, but perhaps unlikely, that a remedy may be introduced by legislation. Recently the Protection of Privacy Bill 1989 was introduced into Parliament by a private member which, although attracting a widespread support in the House of Commons, did not secure government backing and, therefore, failed to reach the statute book. In the absence of legislation, the fashioning of any remedy lies with the courts.

As yet, there is no cause of action based simply upon an

1. E.g. the award of £500,000 to Mr Jeffrey Archer; and the out of court settlement of £1 million to Mr Elton John and the award of £1.5 million to Lord Aldington

invasion of privacy in English law.[2] If any remedy is to be found, it is in the application of the law of confidence. The aim of this paper is to argue that the law of confidence may provide considerable ammunition for a victim of media intrusion into his or her private life.

At the outset of this discussion, one can point to high judicial support for the application of the law of confidence to the protection of privacy. In the course of his speech in the *Spycatcher* case, Lord Keith of Kinkel asserted that "The right to personal privacy is clearly one which the law in this field should protect. If a profit has been made through the revelation in breach of confidence of a person's private life it is appropriate that the profit should be accounted for to that person".[3] To see to what extent these sentiments can operate to protect privacy, it is necessary to examine the basis of the law of confidence and its potential sphere of application.

THE BASIS OF THE LAW OF CONFIDENCE[4]

An obligation of confidentiality can be imposed by a contract. Such an obligation can be imposed by an express contractual term but, even in the absence of such a term, the courts are sympathetically disposed to imply such an obligation.[5] In the present context, however, there may well be no contractual relationship between any of the parties to the litigation. In such circumstances, any obligation of confidence originates in equity.

An early, and influential, decision in the law of confidence was *Prince Albert* v. *Strange*,[6] where the Prince Consort obtained, *inter alia*, an injunction restraining the exhibition of

2. *Bernstein of Leigh (Baron)* v. *Skyviews & General Ltd.* [1978] Q.B. 479; *Malone* v. *The Metropolitan Police Commissioner* [1979] Ch. 334, 350, *per* Sir Robert Megarry V.-C. For an early and penetrating discussion of the American approach, see S.D. Warren and L.D. Brandeis (1890) 4 Harv. L.R. 193.

3. *Attorney-General* v. *Guardian Newspapers (No. 2)* [1988] 3 All E.R. 545, 639–640.

4. For the fullest account, see F. Gurry, *Breach of Confidence, passim.*

5. E.g. *Initial Services Ltd.* v. *Putterill* [1968] 1 Q.B. 396; *Fraser* v. *Thames Television Ltd.* [1983] 2 All E.R. 101; Gurry *op. cit.* pp. 28–29.

6. (1849) 1 Mac. & G. 25. See also *Abernethy* v. *Hutchinson* (1825) 1 H. & T.W. 28; *Morrison* v. *Moat* (1851) 9 Hare 241.

various etchings that he had made. In granting the injunction, various reasons were advanced. These included breach of trust and contract and also that, as Prince Albert had the exclusive property in the etchings, he could restrain their unauthorised use. More importantly, it was also held that the exhibition of the etchings would have amounted to a breach of confidence.

Although there were a number of bases for the decision, the most important was the invocation of the law of confidence. This obligation can arise quite independently of the law of contract, as was illustrated in *Seager* v. *Copydex Ltd.*[7] In this case, the plaintiff, during preliminary negotiations with the defendants, revealed to them secret information about a new type of carpet grip which he had invented. The negotiations broke down but the defendants nevertheless produced a carpet grip of their own. In so doing, however, they made use, albeit unconsciously, of the information imparted to them by the plaintiff. The action for breach of confidence could not be based upon contract because there had never been a contractual relationship between the parties. This supposed difficulty was brushed aside. According to Lord Denning M.R.:

> "The law on this subject does not depend on any implied contract. It depends upon the broad principle of equity that he who receives information in confidence shall not take unfair advantage of it. He must not make use of it to the prejudice of him who gave it without obtaining consent."[8]

This equitable obligation referred to by Lord Denning is well-established. The circumstances in which such an obligation will arise were enumerated by Megarry J. as being that the information must have the requisite degree of secrecy or confidence attached to it and that the information must have been imparted in circumstances in which the confidant ought reasonably to have known that the information had been imparted in confidence.[9] These criteria must be considered in turn.

7. [1967] 1 W.L.R. 923
8. *Ibid.* at p. 931.
9. *Coco* v. *A.N. Clark (Engineers) Ltd.* [1969] R.P.C. 41; *Saltman Engineering Co. Ltd.* v. *Campbell Engineering Co. Ltd.* (1948) 65 R.P.C. 203, [1963] 3 All E.R. 413.

CONFIDENTIALITY OF INFORMATION

The action for breach of confidence probably has the greatest scope in the commercial sphere, where there is an obvious interest in restraining the unauthorised use of commercially sensitive information. Thus, as in *Seager* v. *Copydex*, some confidential information about an invention must necessarily be imparted to a potential developer of it so that the latter can judge adequately whether it is a worthwhile project. Similarly, employers must be able to rely on employees not revealing trade secrets to competitors. While commerce may be the most likely setting for actions of confidence, the action can also extend to personal conduct and information.

In the leading case of *Argyll* v. *Argyll*,[10] the Duke of Argyll proposed to write articles in a national newspaper about his marriage to his former wife, the Duchess of Argyll. She obtained an injunction restraining the publication of secrets relating to her private life, personal affairs and private conduct communicated to him during their marriage. Ungoed-Thomas J., considering that the issue of whether marital confidences were protected by equity concerned every home in the country,[11] held that they were and issued an injunction restraining the Duke and the newspaper[12] from publishing such information.

While *Argyll* v. *Argyll* provides clear authority that the law of confidence may be used to preserve marital confidences, it could not be assumed that non-marital or extra-marital confidences would be similarly protected. The early signs that protection would be afforded were unpropitious. In the unsatisfactory decision in *Woodward* v. *Hutchins*,[13] the former press agent of various pop stars had contracted with a daily newspaper to write a series of articles about aspects of their private lives and personal affairs. After an expedited hearing, heard in the late afternoon, the Court of Appeal discharged the interlocutory

10. [1967] Ch. 302. *Cf. Lennon* v. *News Group Newspapers Ltd.* [1978] F.S.R. 573.
11. *Ibid.* at p. 317.
12. This issue is considered below.
13. [1977] 1 W.L.R. 760. For a critical reaction to this decision, see R. Goff and G. Jones, *The Law of Restitution* (3rd ed.), p. 678 and *Castrol Australia Pty. Ltd.* v. *Em-Tech Associates Pty. Ltd.* (1981) 33 A.L.R. 31, 54–57.

injunctions that had been issued earlier in the day. In reaching this conclusion, various strands of reasoning were employed.

One ground was that those who seek and welcome publicity so long as it showed them in a favourable light could not complain about invasions of privacy which showed them in an unfavourable light.[14] This was partly justified upon the basis that the public interest required disclosure; a line which is now difficult to support in the light of the modern approach to this defence to an action for breach of confidence.[15] An alternative reason for refusing injunctive relief was that an interlocutory injunction would not be granted to restrain an alleged libel, which the defendant intended to justify. This also can be criticised, however, in that it confuses the different bases of the two actions[16]

Perhaps the most acceptable rationale of the decision is that much of the information complained of related to matters in the public domain[17] and such information is outside the law of confidence.[18] Indeed, some of the incidents to be recounted occurred in a public place and if due care is not taken to preserve secrecy of conduct or information, no injunction should lie to prevent further dissemination of the information.[19] Nevertheless, the decision did seem to represent an unsympathetic attitude to using the law of confidence to protect the secrecy of aspects of one's personal life.

A rather different and, it is submitted, preferable approach was recently taken, however, in *Stephens* v. *Avery*.[20] The plaintiff and the first defendant were formerly close friends who freely discussed personal matters on the express basis that what the plaintiff told her friend was secret and disclosed in confidence. The first defendant, however, passed on to a newspaper details of the plaintiff's sexual conduct, including details of a lesbian affair that the plaintiff had had with a Mrs. Telling, who had recently been murdered by her husband. After this story had

14. [1977] 1 W.L.R. at p. 764, *per* Lord Denning M.R., at p. 675, *per* Bridge L. J.
15. *Infra*.
16. *Infra*.
17. See also *Khashoggi* v. *Smith* (1980) 124 S.J. 149.
18. *Attorney-General* v. *Guardian Newspapers (No. 2), supra*.
19. See G. Jones (1970) 86 L.Q.R. 476, 482.
20. [1988] 2 All E.R. 477.

been published, the plaintiffs sought damages for breach of confidence and the defendants sought to have the action struck out.

Sir Nicolas Browne-Wilkinson V.-C. refused to strike the action out. Although he took the view that the courts would not enforce a duty of confidence relating to matters of a grossly immoral tendency, information relating to sexual conduct could be the subject of a legally enforceable duty of confidence if it would be unconscionable for a person who had received that information to reveal it to another. This was particularly the case on the present facts where there had been an express promise of secrecy. Neither did the Vice-Chancellor regard the information as being trivial tittle-tattle which could not be the subject matter of confidentiality, expressing the greatest doubt that it could be described thus.[21] He therefore held that the action should go to trial.

This decision, although only a striking-out action, is important. It rightly regards information pertaining to a person's personal conduct to be capable of being protected by the law of confidence. In this instance, the conduct was of a sexual nature. This may not necessarily be the case. Lord Keith, in the *Spycatcher* case, instanced as another example a donor to a worthy cause being entitled to have any desired anonymity protected by the law of confidence.[22] Again, to take an example given by the Law Commission,[23] the very fact that a secret meeting had occurred should be capable of being the subject matter of confidentiality, let alone what was said. In short, there is no reason in principle why personal behaviour of various types should not be within the ambit of the law of confidence. What is rather more problematic is to consider the situations when the obligation of confidentiality can arise and against whom it can be enforced.

THE EXTENT OF AN OBLIGATION OF CONFIDENCE

To date, the discussion has centred on what type of information can come within the ambit of the law of confidence. Rather

21. *Ibid.* at p. 481.

22. *Attorney-General* v. *Guardian Newspapers (No. 2)* [1988] 3 All E.R. 545, 640.

23. Law Com. No. 110 (1981) p. 133.

more attention now needs to be paid to the question of against whom the obligation can be enforced and, in particular, the circumstances in which a person who is not privy to the relationship of confidentiality, if any, can himself become subject to an obligation of confidence.

It has long been accepted that where A owes a duty of confidence to B and, in breach of that duty, A imparts that information to C, C may also be subject, in equity, to an action for breach of confidence.[24] Thus, for example, in *Argyll* v. *Argyll* the newspaper to whom the confidential information had been given was restrained from publishing it. Were the position otherwise, a confidant could effectively remove the obligation of confidentiality by wrongly disclosing the information to a third party, which would deprive the law of confidentiality of any content.[25] Subject only to the qualification that if A's breach of confidence causes the information to enter the public domain,[26] a recipient of the information who has notice[27] of its confidential nature will come under an obligation of confidentiality. This is straightforward. What is less clear is whether an obligation of confidentiality can arise when there has been no voluntary revelation of information but the information has been acquired by intrusive means such as telephone tapping or the use of telephoto lens photography.

Some commentators take the view that to impose a duty of confidence in these circumstances is to confuse confidence, which the law does protect, with privacy, which the law does not.[28] *Dicta* in *Malone* v. *The Metropolitan Police Commissioner*[29] support this view. In this case, the plaintiff sought a declaration that the tapping of his telephone by the police had been unlawful and an injunction to restrain the future interception or monitoring

24. *Prince Albert* v. *Strange, supra.*

25. *Attorney-General* v. *Guardian Newspapers (No. 2)* [1988] 3 All E.R. 545, 644, *per* Lord Keith.

26. *Attorney-General* v. *Guardian Newspapers (No. 2) supra* at p. 652, *per* Lord Griffiths.

27. *Attorney-General* v. *Guardian Newspapers (No. 2) supra* at p. 658, *per* Lord Goff. See also Gurry *op. cit.* pp. 286–289.

28. See R. Wacks, *The Protection of Privacy*, pp. 9–11; Law Com. No. 110 pp. 5–6 and the comments in Chapter 1. For different views, see Gurry *op. cit.* pp. 164–165; Jones *loc. cit.* p. 482.

29. [1979] Ch. 334. See C. Harlow [1980] P.L. 1.

of conversations on his line. In refusing relief, Sir Robert Megarry V.-C. held that this activity by the police was not unlawful.[30] However he went on to express the view that there would be no remedy to a person who had had his telephone tapped by a private individual. This was not, however, because of the absence of a confidential relationship; rather, the Vice-Chancellor thought that if one used a telephone, there is an inherent risk of being overheard. Because one runs the risk of a crossed line, he thought one must also run the risk of an eavesdropper.

With respect, this approach seems to be difficult to defend and the authorities which consider the unauthorised acquisition of information are against it. Thus in *Ashburton* v. *Pape*,[31] in granting an injunction to restrain the use of privileged documents acquired by deception, Swinfen Eady J. said that:

> "The principle upon which the Court of Chancery has acted for many years has been to restrain the publication of confidential information *improperly or surreptitously obtained* or of information imparted in confidence which ought not be divulged."[32]

Equally explicit is the Australian decision in *Franklin* v. *Giddins*.[33] The plaintiff had, by a secret method of cross-breeding, produced a new type of tree. The defendant stole a specimen and thereby discovered the previously secret genetic structure of the wood. The plaintiff succeeded in an action for breach of confidence. Dunn J. emphatically rejected the argument that there must be a prior relationship of confidence between A and B before one could be liable to the other for breach of confidence. He was "quite unable to accept that a thief who steals a trade secret, with the intention of using it in commercial competition with its owner, to the detriment of the latter, and so uses it, is less unconscionable than a traitorous servant."[34]

The approach of Sir Robert Megarry V.-C. was not followed in the important Court of Appeal decision in *Francome* v. *Mirror*

30. See now Interception of Communications Act 1985.
31. [1913] 2 Ch. 469; *Tournier* v. *National Provincial and Union Bank of England* [1924] 1 K.B. 461.
32. [1913] 2 Ch. 469, 475. Emphasis supplied.
33. [1978] 1 Qd. R. 72. See W. J. Braithwaite (1979) 95 L.Q.R. 323.
34. *Ibid.* at p. 80.

Group Newspapers Ltd.[35] The defendants had acquired, from an undisclosed source, a number of tapes of telephone conversations between the plaintiffs, a leading National Hunt jockey and his wife. It was alleged that these tapes revealed breaches by Mr Francome of both the Jockey Club rules and, more seriously the criminal law. On being informed by the defendants that they intended to publish, the plaintiffs sought and obtained interlocutory injunctions restraining them from so doing; the basis of the action being a breach of confidence. The Court of Appeal considered there to be a serious issue to be tried that the eavesdropper was under a duty of confidentiality with regard to the telephone conversations and that the defendants, who knew how the tapes had been acquired, were under a similar obligation.

These decisions place little emphasis on the notion of one person giving information to a confidant. Rather the focus is on the protection of information that is secret. That this is so emerges from the speech of Lord Goff of Chieveley in the *Spycatcher* case. Lord Goff, after referring to situations where a duty of confidence arises in equity where there has been a disclosure of information, said that such a duty would also arise "where an obviously confidential document is wafted by an electric fan out of a window into a crowded street, or when an obviously confidential document, such as a private diary, is dropped in a public place, and is then picked up by a passer-by."[36]

The early emphasis in breach of confidence actions was to protect the secrecy of information confided by one person to another. As the examples given by Lord Goff indicate, the law seems to be moving beyond this, to afford protection to secret information which may not have been confided to anyone. The example of the private diary is a particularly good illustration of this, in that such diaries are often intended to be read only by the author of them. Clearly, there is no pre-existing confidential relationship, yet because the information is secret, the law of confidentiality can, as Lord Goff made clear, extend to it.

The development of the law of confidence in this way offers

35. [1984] 2 All E.R. 408.
36. [1988] 3 All E.R. 545, 658–659.

considerable scope for it to protect personal privacy. In particular, matters such as personal relations and behaviour, health and personal communications[37] should clearly in principle be capable of protection by the law of confidence. The difficulty stems from ascertaining the circumstances in which such a duty will arise when a person discovers such information for himself rather than having it revealed to him in confidence.

The key to solving this problem, it is suggested, lies simply in considering whether the person who acquires the information ought reasonably to know that it is secret. If, for example, a couple conduct a liaison in public places then it is difficult to see that there could be any obligation of confidentiality imposed upon any observer. Where, however, the observer has made some effort to elicit the information, then a stronger case can be made for regarding it as being within the law of confidence.

In developing this argument one can usefully consider variations of the facts of *Avery* v. *Stephens*[38] where, it will be recalled, the existence of a lesbian relationship revealed to a friend was regarded as within the law of confidence. If this information had been discovered by normal observation of the parties at public occasions then it is hard to see that it would have the necessary secrecy to be regarded as confidential. Suppose, however, that the friend had not been told of the relationship but had discovered it by spying on the plaintiff who thought she was conducting her affair in secret. This seems much the same in principle to the action of the telephone tapper in *Francome* v. *Mirror Group Newspapers Ltd.* and, it is submitted, a duty of confidence should arise. A workable test in this context might be to consider whether the person acquiring the information has had to adopt investigative techniques, such as artificial aids or the use of vantage points, to discover what is going on.[39] The fact that these measures need to be resorted to might suggest that the person observed is seeking to conduct his affairs in secret. Provided the information actually is secret, then, it is argued, the investigator should be under a duty of confidence with regard to what has been observed.

37. *Cf.* Protection of Privacy Bill 1989, cl. 7.
38. [1988] 2 All E.R. 477.
39. *Cf.* Law Com. No. 110, p. 116.

PUBLIC INTEREST[40]

Should the argument in favour of extending the law of confidence to cover situations frequently perceived as aspects of privacy be accepted, a remaining issue, before considering the available remedies, is that of the public interest in disclosure; a consideration which has always acted to qualify any obligation of confidentiality.

The public interest qualification to the duty of confidence is frequently, if inaccurately, referred to as the "iniquity rule".[41] The basis of this qualification is that one cannot rely on the law of confidentiality to protect the secrecy of misconduct. Thus in *Initial Services Ltd.* v. *Putterill*,[42] where it was alleged that the company had both acted in breach of the Restrictive Trade Practices Act 1956 and also misled their customers as to the reason for a price increase this information could not be protected by the law of confidence.

Although this case concerned misconduct, the exception to the duty of confidence is wider than this. The true principle is simply to consider whether it is in the public interest that certain information be made public.[43] This necessarily vague doctrine tends to relate to matters which are harmful to the public such as an impending disaster.[44] On this basis information supplied in confidence by leaders of the Church of Scientology to adherents of that sect has been held not to be protected by the law of confidence, because the evidence showed that the tenets of this "religion" were harmful to the public.[45] Similarly, secret information relating to drugs that are harmful to the public may not be protected, if the product remains on the market.[46]

This principle was applied in *Woodward* v. *Hutchins*,[47]

40. For the fullest discussion of this, see Y. Cripps (1984) 40 J.L.S. 361.
41. *Gartside* v. *Outram* (1857) 26 L.J.Ch. 113.
42. [1968] 1 Q.B. 396.
43. *Fraser* v. *Evans* [1969] 1 Q.B. 349, 362, *per* Lord Denning M.R.
44. *Malone* v. *The Metropolitan Police Commissioner* [1979] Ch. 344, 362, *per* Megarry V.-C.
45. *Hubbard* v. *Vosper* [1972] 2 Q.B. 84; *Church of Scientology of California* v. *Kaufman* [1973] R.P.C. 635.
46. *Cf. Distillers Co. Ltd.* v. *Times Newspapers Ltd.* [1975] Q.B. 613; *Schering Chemicals Ltd.* v. *Falkman* [1982] Q.B. 1.
47. [1977] 1 W.L.R. 760.

where Lord Denning M.R. expressed the view that as the plaintiffs had actively sought to present themselves in a favourable light, it was in the public interest that the true picture should emerge; that public interest outweighing any obligation of confidence owed to them by their press agent. This approach to the public interest defence has always seemed somewhat dubious; in the light of recent judicial treatment of this matter, however, it seems untenable.

In *Francome* v. *Mirror Group Newspapers Ltd.*[48] it was strenuously argued, that given the serious nature of the allegations, it was in the public interest that the information be published. Sir John Donaldson M.R., however, expressed the view that the press are particularly vulnerable to the error of confusing the public interest with their own interest. He could not see how the public interest would not be equally well served by giving the information to the Jockey Club or to the police as by publishing it to the whole world.[49]

This approach to the public interest defence is to be welcomed, in that it reinforces the obligation of confidence, while enabling cases of wrongdoing to be reported to the proper authorities.[50] This approach, coupled with an increased willingness to consider critically what is alleged to be in the public interest to disclose,[51] should surely mean that it will be increasingly difficult to argue that the revelation of the details of a person's private life is in the public interest. While no doubt the public, or sections of it, are interested in reading such stories, that is not to say it is in the public interest for them to be published.

In addition to the public interest qualification to the law of confidence being more narrowly defined than in the past, the courts also seem unwilling to accept that extra-marital sexual behaviour is so immoral as to be outwith the law of confidence. Such an argument was raised by the defendants in *Stephens* v. *Avery*[52] in terms that a lesbian relationship was immoral

48. [1984] 2 All E.R. 408.
49. *Ibid.* at p. 413.
50. See also *Attorney-General* v. *Guardian Newspapers (No. 2)* [1988] 3 All E.R. 545, 659–660, *per* Lord Goff. *Cf. Lion Laboratories Ltd.* v. *Evans* [1984] 2 All E.R. 417 for a rare exception to this principle.
51. See *British Steel Corporation* v. *Granada Television Ltd.* [1981] A.C. 1096, 1169, *per* Lord Wilberforce.
52. [1988] 2 All E.R. 477.

and so its secrecy could not be protected by the equitable doctrine of confidentiality. This argument was elegantly refuted by Sir Nicolas Browne-Wilkinson V.-C., who pointed out that "The sexual conduct of the plaintiff was not so morally shocking ... as to prevent the third defendant, a major national Sunday newspaper, from spreading the story all over its front and inside pages".[53] It would seem, therefore, that individuals may well have recourse to this branch of the law to protect the privacy of their personal lives.

This is not to say that there will not be instances when the public interest cannot legitimately be relied upon to justify the revelation of a person's private life. If, for example, a person is involved in a campaign to raise public morals but is himself involved in immoral behaviour, it would seem unlikely that he could rely on the law of confidence to prevent exposure as a hypocrite.[54] It should not be the case, however, that simply because a person is prominent in one field or another he should be without remedy if his private life is exposed. It remains to be considered what remedies are available in this sphere for breach of confidence.

REMEDIES

Of most concern to a person seeking to protect the privacy of his private life is the prevention of that material entering the public domain. If he has advance notice that publication is to take place, an interlocutory injunction is clearly the most appropriate remedy. At one time, it was unclear whether the principles established in *American Cyanamid Co.* v. *Ethicon*[55] applied to an action to restrain publication in breach of confidence. This uncertainty stemmed from a supposed analogy with libel cases[56] where, because of the interest of free speech, interlocutory injunctions are not granted when the defendant intends

53. *Ibid.* at p. 480.
54. *Cf.* the affair of the evangelist Jimmy Swaggart in the U.S.A.
55. [1975] A.C. 396.
56. *Woodward* v. *Hutchins* [1977] 1 W.L.R. 760, 764, *per* Lord Denning M.R.; 765, *per* Lawton and Bridge L.JJ.

to justify what is to be published.[57] The perceived analogy is now seen to be false, in this context, in that a breach of confidence action presupposes that the information is true, whereas in a libel action, the complaint is that it is false.[58] The previous uncertainty has now been dispelled[59] and it is now clear that the principles of *American Cyanamid* are applicable.[60]

In assessing where the balance of convenience lies, it is thought that in virtually all cases, it will be in favour of granting relief. If the defendant is permitted to publish pending a trial, the damage will be done and the information public; the genie cannot be put back into the bottle. On the other hand, if for some reason the plaintiff cannot establish a duty of confidence, the defendant has merely been delayed in publishing the story. Such a consideration weighed heavily with the majority in the interlocutory proceedings in the *Spycatcher* case[61] and, it is submitted, should in general favour the grant of an injunction.

PECUNIARY REMEDIES

It may well be that the first the plaintiff knows of the breach of confidence is when he sees the information has been published. Any remedy then will inevitably be of a pecuniary nature as an injunction would clearly be pointless. The first option is to seek an account of profits.[62] This remedy is available to divest the defendant of the money he has made by the misuse of the confidential information and is of most use in the commercial context. In *Peter Pan Manufacturing Corp.* v. *Corsets Silhouette Ltd.*[63] the defendants had, in breach of confidence, used the plaintiffs' design to manufacture a new style of brassiere. One

57. *Bonnard* v. *Perryman* [1891] 2 Ch. 269; *Fraser* v. *Evans* [1969] 1 Q.B. 349; *Bestobell Paints Ltd.* v. *Bigg* [1975] F.S.R. 421; *Harakas* v. *Baltic Exchange* [1982] 2 All E.R. 701.

58. *Khashoggi* v. *Smith* (1980) 124 S.J. 149. See also P. H. Pettit, *Equity and the Law of Trusts* (5th ed.), p. 488; Goff and Jones *op. cit.* p. 678.

59. See A. Boyle [1982] P.L. 574, 580–585.

60. *Francome* v. *Mirror Group Newspapers Ltd.*, *supra.*

61. *Attorney-General* v. *Guardian Newspapers Ltd.* [1987] 1 W.L.R. 1248.

62. See F.E. Patfield (1987) 11 Adelaide L.R. 1.

63. [1968] 1 W.L.R. 809.

of the remedies granted was an order that the defendants account to the plaintiff for the profits made during manufacture.

In the commercial context, it is relatively easy to identify the profit which is attributable to the misuse of information. In the context of publication by the media of private information, this task is more difficult. Unless there is a clear increase of circulation which can be attributed to the offending story, it will be difficult for a plaintiff to be able to identify which part of the proceeds represents the unjust enrichment derived from the breach of confidence. Thus despite the government being entitled to an account in the *Spycatcher* case, it is not likely that this remedy will be much used. A preferable line of attack is simply to claim damages. There are, however, two potential difficulties in awarding damages. First is the question of whether damages can be awarded at all and, secondly, if so, upon what basis they are to be assessed. These matters will be considered in turn.

In *Seager* v. *Copydex Ltd.*[64] the Court of Appeal held that the remedy of account was inappropriate and instead ordered an enquiry as to damages. In *Seager* v. *Copydex (No. 2) Ltd.*[65] these damages were assessed by analogy with the tort of conversion on the basis of what a willing purchaser would have paid a willing vendor for the information. What was not explained was the basis on which damages could be awarded at all.

Academic opinion has favoured the view that the basis upon which damages were awarded was under Lord Cairns' Act.[66] As the court could have restrained further use of the information by injunction, damages could be awarded in lieu of it.[67] If this is correct, however, no damages could be awarded for publication of personal information. As the material cannot be "unpublished", there is no jurisdiction to grant an injunction and so no power to award damages in lieu. Alternatively, the basis of the award could be that the information is itself property and the misuse of it amounts to the tort of conversion. The

64. [1967] 1 W.L.R. 923.
65. [1969] 1 W.L.R. 809.
66. Chancery Amendment Act 1858. See now Supreme Court Act 1981, s. 50.
67. Gurry *op. cit.* p. 430; G. Forai (1971) 6 Syd. L.R. 382, 392–393. See also *Attorney-General* v. *Guardian Newspapers Ltd. (No. 2)* [1988] 3 All E.R. 545, 662, *per* Lord Goff.

problem with this, however, is quite simply that information is not generally regarded as property.[68] It certainly cannot be stolen[69] and it is doubtful if it can be converted.

The remaining possibility is that the court can simply award damages for breach of an equitable obligation.[70] This is regarded by some as theoretically controversial,[71] yet it is not a point which seems to have troubled the courts, it simply being assumed that damages can be awarded.[72] On the basis that the courts can award damages, the remaining issue to consider is how they should be assessed.

The basis of an award of damages seems to be accepted as being tortious.[73] In the commercial context, this involves, as shown in *Seager* v. *Copydex (No. 2)*, assessing the value of the information. In the context of personal information, this presents a rather greater difficulty. The damages caused in these cases is the distress occasioned by the public revelation of one's private life. As such, the best analogy would appear to be with libel where damages are available to compensate for distress.[74] The quantification of such damages would, of course, be in the hands of a judge rather than, as is the case with libel, a jury.

CONCLUSIONS

Not all would agree that the development of the law of confidence along the lines advocated in this paper would be desirable. It could be argued that any such development would amount to a muzzling of the press and would stem from a confusion between confidence and privacy. Nevertheless, it does seem that

68. *Boardman* v. *Phipps* [1967] 2 A.C. 46, 127–128, *per* Lord Upjohn. See also J. E. Stuckey (1918) 9 Syd. L.R. 402, and Chapter 5.

69. *Oxford* v. *Moss* (1978) 68 Cr.App.Rep. 183.

70. This excludes the possibility that there is a nominate tort of breach of confidence. *Cf.* Street, *Torts* (8th ed.), p. 6.

71. See f.n. 67 *supra*

72. *Fraser* v. *Thames Television Ltd.* [1983] 2 All E.R. 101. See Goff and Jones *op. cit.* pp. 672–673.

73. *General Tire and Rubber Co.* v. *Firestone Tyre and Rubber Co. Ltd.* [1975] 1 W.L.R. 819, 824, *per* Lord Wilberforce; Goff and Jones *op. cit.* p. 672.

74. *Goslin* v. *Corry* (1844) 7 M. & G. 342; *Ley* v. *Hamilton* (1935) 153 L.T. 384.

recent case-law has shown that the courts are willing to extend the law of confidence in this way. It is submitted that this is a desirable development.

It was noted at the outset that there has been increased concern at the intrusive behaviour of the media and, in particular, certain sections of the press. While recent moves towards self-regulation by the press are to be welcomed, it nevertheless seems right that the law should also afford protection to aggrieved individuals. It is surely not unreasonable for a person to expect that what he does in private should, as a general rule, remain private. Still less should he have to endure close, and perhaps intrusive, surveillance for the purpose of providing material for a story which may amount to little more than salacious gossip.

In the absence of a cognate right of privacy,[75] the law of confidence seems the best weapon to use to prevent practices such as those described. It is to be hoped, therefore, that the signs that the law is moving down this road are correct and that it becomes generally recognised that the law of confidence has a major role to play in the protection of privacy.

MARK THOMPSON

75. *Cf.* D. Siepp (1983) 3 O.J.L.S. 325, 370.

CHAPTER 5

INFORMATION AS PROPERTY

INTRODUCTION

The object of this chapter is to examine two principal questions: can information constitute property, and does the protection of information benefit from such a classification?

The second question is important for two reasons. First, most Commonwealth legal systems already possess a developed law of confidentiality. It might, therefore, be argued that to classify information rights as property would add nothing to their protection: the law works adequately as it is, and a proprietary analysis could serve merely to complicate the issue. Secondly, the common law generally over-uses its concept of property. An example is the law of sale of goods, where the Sale of Goods Act 1979, having gone to great lengths to identify the owner, proceeds to neutralise many of the more inconvenient consequences of this identification.[1] It would be unfortunate if a similar ambiguity became a characteristic of our law of confidential information.

There is substance in each of these objections. Indeed, one reason why the Law Commission[2] rejected an analogy with property as the most constructive avenue of development was that the present law of confidence had already developed along

1. See ss. 16–25 of the Act, discussed by Atiyah, *Sale of Goods* (8th ed.), pp. 281–287 *et seq.*; Smith, *Property Problems in Sale*, *passim*. In answering such questions as the identification of priorities upon insolvency, for instance, there is much to be said for the "specific issue" approach taken by the Uniform Commercial Code, as against the simplistic search for the property-holder which is required by English law.

2. *Breach of Confidence*, Report No. 110, Cmnd. 8388, 1981, para. 2.10. But *cf.* Kearney, *The Action for Breach of Confidence in Australia*, at p. 35.

largely non-proprietary lines; the introduction of notions of property at this stage could therefore distort existing principles.

Another complicating factor is the peculiar quality of information. Although intangible, it is normally recorded in tangible form. This raises questions as to how far interests in the tangible record can be separated from those attaching to the information alone. Moreover, if rights in tangibly-recorded information can be vindicated by means of an action for trespass or conversion relating to the record itself,[3] it might seem absurd for the law to offer discriminatory remedies where the information does not exist tangibly (for example, where a customer list is merely memorised).[4] Lord Radcliffe, in a tax case, has described know-how as a form of corporate asset *sui generis* because it can be used repeatedly by its proprietor without necessarily depleting its value.[5] On the other hand, its disclosure to unauthorised parties can dilute its value irremediably, rendering worthless any claim for restitution of the mere information itself. Such characteristics clearly demand a measure of differential treatment; some would argue that the level of specialist analysis required is so pronounced as to justify dropping the proprietary label altogether.

Even so, there may also be benefits in recruiting, if not adopting outright, concepts drawn from our law of personal property to answer questions about civil law of protection of information. Such an exercise would, at least, extend the repertoire of legal analogies available to courts when they are required to decide new issues in the law of information, and would enable judicial innovations to be derived from established comparators, rather than merely synthesised in the dark.

The principal area in which this comparison might be helpful is probably that of remedies.[6] If principles akin to those governing the measure of damages for conversion of a chattel can be

3. *Thurston* v. *Charles* (1905) 21 T.L.R. 659; *British Steel Corpn.* v. *Granada Television Ltd.* [1981] A.C. 1096, at p. 1105, *per* Megarry V.-C.; *Borden Chemical Co. (Canada) Ltd.* v. *J.G. Beukers Ltd.* (1973) 29 D.L.R. (3d) 337.

4. *Olschewski* v. *Hudson*, 87 Cal. App. 282, 262 Pac. 43 (1927); *Mackay* v. *Benjamin Franklin Co.*, 288 Pa. 207, 135 Atl. 613 (1927). For the facts, see Palmer, *Bailment* (2nd ed.), Chapter 3.

5. *Rolls-Royce Ltd.* v. *Jeffrey* [1962] 1 All E.R. 801 at p. 805.

6. Stuckey, *The Equitable Action for Breach of Confidence: Is Information Ever Property?* (1981) 9 Syd. L.R. 402 at pp. 415 *et seq.*

applied to claims for the misappropriation of confidential information,[7] the analogy might be developed along other dimensions suggested by the law of wrongful interference with goods. In cases, for example, of information which possesses a peculiar or personal significance, and for the misappropriation of which damages would be an inadequate remedy, a court might be persuaded to grant special damages to represent distress occasioned by the disclosure,[8] or injunctive relief akin to an order for specific restitution available for the tort of detinue at common law.[9]

But analogies from the law of tangible personalty might also prove helpful in establishing (or negating) original duties.[10] If, for example, the principles which govern possessory relations over chattels could be adapted to the entrustment of information, the results might cast useful light on the obligations of a "finder" of confidential information,[11] or of a party who comes involuntarily into possession of it,[12] or of a party who (innocently or otherwise) improves it; they might also clarify the capacity of the entrustee to question the entruster's right to the information or to sue third parties who interfere with it. Such comparisons may appear far-fetched, but there is at least one modern

7. *Seager* v. *Copydex (No. 2)* [1969] 1 W.L.R. 809 C.A.; see below.

8. Cf. *Harris* v. *Lombard New Zealand Ltd.* [1974] 2 N.Z.L.R. 161 at pp. 169, 170; *Ichard* v. *Frangoulis* [1977] 2 All E.R. 461; *Millar* v. *Candy* (1981) 58 F.L.R. 145; *Graham* v. *Voigt* (1989) 95 F.L.R. 146 (tortious deprivation of, or damage to, chattel; damages for loss of enjoyment awarded).

9. Stuckey, *op. cit.*

10. Indeed, in certain cases a straightforward action for the infringement of legal property in tangibles would appear to offer a more direct and appropriate form of redress than equitable notions of confidence. The classic modern instance is *Franklin* v. *Giddins* [1978] Qd. R. 72, where the defendant's plagiarism of a unique strain of nectarine, which the plaintiff had spent over 15 years developing, was preceded by his stealing four twigs of the plaintiff's budwood under cover of night. Notwithstanding the fact that this case contained a strong element of the violation of common law property in tangible material, and could perhaps have been disposed of on the basis of a waiver of tort, Dunn J. appears to have grounded his decision on a breach of the equitable duty of confidence. See further Stuckey (1981) 9 Syd. L.R. 402 at pp. 429–430; Cornish, *Intellectual Property* (2nd ed.), p. 233.

11. *Cf.* the observations of Donaldson L.J. in *Parker* v. *British Airways Board* [1982] Q.B. 1004 at p. 1007 (finder of chattel must take reasonable steps to reunite chattel with owner and take reasonable care of it meanwhile); and see the *Guardian* case (below), at pp. 658–659, *per* Lord Goff of Chieveley.

12. *Cf.* Cornish, *op. cit.*, p. 226.

example of the invocation of bailment principles to illuminate an issue of confidential information. In *Attorney-General* v. *Guardian Newspapers Ltd (No. 2)*,[13] Lord Goff of Chieveley drew the comparison when considering whether an original obligation of confidence imposed on a repository of confidential information continued to affect that repository, notwithstanding his prior release of the confidential information into the public domain. His Lordship remarked:

> "I have to say ... that I know of no case (apart from the present) in which the maxim [*that no man shall be allowed to profit from his own wrong*] has been invoked in order to hold that a person under an obligation is not released from that obligation by the destruction of the subject matter of the obligation, on the ground that the destruction was the result of his own wrongful act. To take an obvious example, a bailee who by his own wrongful, even deliberately wrongful, act destroys the goods entrusted to him, is obviously relieved of his obligation as bailee, though he is of course liable in damages for the tort."

A more specific comparison might be made in regard to consumer protection. If, as appears self-evident, commodities such as "know-how" and computer software can be marketed, it might seem logical to derive the supplier's obligations as to the acquirer's exclusivity of use and security of tenure, and as to the quality and suitability of the intangible information itself, from principles applicable to the commercial supply of tangible commodities.[14] This could involve, for example, implying into the relevant transaction terms analogous to those implied by the Sale of Goods Act 1979 and the Supply of Goods and Services Act 1982.

13. [1988] 3 All E.R. 545 at p. 662 (H.L.); but *cf*. at p. 664, where Lord Goff finally left the question open, reflecting that "cases of breach of confidence may well involve questions of property (in particular, copyright) as well as questions of personal liability"; and that "in a case involving national security ... the guilty confidant may be liable to criminal prosecution. It is only if we take these matters into account that we can see such a case in the round." For criticism of Lord Goff's analysis of the position of the bailee, see Palmer, *Bailment* (2nd ed.), Chapter 1.

14. Below, p. 103.

AUTHORITY FAVOURING THE PROPRIETARY ANALYSIS

There is no shortage of modern authority accepting that certain categories of information can, in principle, constitute property. The possibility was recognised by three of their Lordships in *Boardman* v. *Phipps*.[15] In *Markwell Bros* v. *CPN Diesels*,[16] the court extended the classification to the point of holding that a company set up by former employee-directors of the plaintiff company held confidential information received from them on constructive trusteeship for its rightful owner, who could recover "equitable damages" for the misuse of the information as an alternative to an action for account. In *Rolls-Royce Ltd* v. *Jeffrey*[17] Lord Radcliffe saw no objection to treating "know-how" as a corporate asset distinct from the physical records in which it was contained: "It is intangible; but then so is goodwill." In *Herbert Morris Ltd* v. *Saxelby*[18] Lord Shaw of Dunfermline remarked bluntly that: "Trade secrets . . . may not be taken away by a servant; they are his master's property . . ." In *Exchange Telegraph* v. *Gregory*[19] the Court of Appeal accepted that the plaintiff had a right of property in certain Stock Exchange information (for which he had paid the Stock Exchange Committee) sufficient to entitle him to an injunction restraining the

15. [1967] 2 A.C. 46 at pp. 89–91 (Viscount Dilhorne), 107–111 (Lord Hodson), 115–116 (Lord Guest, who remarked that he saw no reason why information and knowledge could not constitute the property of a trust). And see further *(SC) Surveys and Mining Ltd.* v. *Morrison* [1969] Qd. S.R. 470 at pp. 473–474, *per* W.B. Campbell J.

16. [1983] Qd. R. 508. See further *Technograph Printed Circuits Ltd.* v. *Chalwyn Ltd.* [1967] R.P.C. 339 at p. 344, where Plowman J. referred to the plaintiffs' "proprietary interests by way of confidential information for which they are entitled to protection"; *Searle & Co. Ltd.* v. *Celltech Ltd.* [1982] F.S.R. 92 at p. 105; and the further authorities cited by Gurry, *Breach of Confidence*, p. 46 fn. 25.

17. [1962] 1 All E.R. 801, 805; see also *Evans Medical Supplies Ltd.* v. *Moriarty* (1956–1957) 37 Tax Cas. 540; *Musker* v. *English Electric Co. Ltd.* (1964) 41 Tax Cas. 556.

18. [1916] 1 A.C. 688, at p. 714; see also *B.O. Morris Ltd.* v. *Gilman* (1943) 60 R.P.C. 20; *Yates Circuit Foil Co. Ltd.* v. *Electrofoils Ltd.* [1976] F.S.R. 345 at pp. 384–385, *per* Whitford J.; *Drake Personnel Ltd.* v. *Beddison* [1979] V.R. 13, at p. 22, *per* Anderson J.

19. [1896] 1 Q.B. 147.

defendants from misusing it.[20] In *Dean* v. *MacDowell*[21] Cotton J. accepted that the phrase "any property of the partnership" should be taken to include any information "which the partnership is entitled to"; an interpretation which was endorsed and refined by Bowen L.J. in *Aas* v. *Benham*.[22] In *Re Keene*[23] Lord Sterndale held that formulae for the manufacture of products, known only to members of a partnership, constituted partnership property (evidently in much the same way as trade secrets in general) and could pass to its proprietor's trustee in bankruptcy.[24] These and comparable decisions have led Shepherd[25] to conclude unequivocally that "Confidential information is a species of property".

QUALIFICATIONS UPON THE PROPRIETARY ANALYSIS

Few would deny that this is a significant body of authority. And yet, in other quarters, the universal characterisation of information as property has been variously condemned as misleading and otiose. One of its principal critics is Stuckey,[26] who considers the property analysis "juristically misguided and unhelpful" as a medium for interpreting liability for breach of confidence. In Stuckey's view, "The action for breach of confidence, when not based on implied or express contractual obligation, enforces purely equitable obligations arising out of a

20. See also *Exchange Telegraph* v. *Howard* (1906) 22 T.L.R. 375.
21. (1878) 8 Ch.D. 345, 354.
22. [1891] 2 Ch. 244, 255; see also *Bell Houses Ltd.* v. *City Wall Properties Ltd.* [1966] 2 W.L.R. 1323 at pp. 1332–1333, *per* Danckwerts L.J.
23. [1922] 2 Ch. 475.
24. See also *Canham* v. *Jones* (1813) V. & B. 218 (disposed by will); *Bryson* v. *Whitehead* (1823) 1 Sim. & Stu. 74; *Green* v. *Folgham* (1823) 1 Sim. & Stu. 398.
25. *Law of Fiduciaries*, p. 319; and see Ricketson, "Confidential Information—A New Proprietary Interest?" (1977) 11 (No. 2) Melb. Univ. L.R. 223 at p. 225; Weinreb, "Information and Property" (1988) 28 U. Toronto L.J. 177; Kearney, *The Action for Breach of Confidence in Australia*, at pp. 32–36. For further valuable analyses of the identity of information as property, see Gurry, *Breach of Confidence*, pp. 46–56 and Birks, *Introduction to the Law of Restitution*, pp. 343–344, both cited by Lord Goff of Chieveley in the *Guardian* case (above) at p. 659.
26. (1981) 9 Syd. L.R. 402, at p. 404.

proven relationship of trust, not property rights in information."[27]

In the light of such criticisms, it is submitted that the preceding authority must be qualified in at least three respects.

First, it does not necessarily establish a universal characterisation of information as property. Rather, it might be taken to suggest a similarity of treatment in certain limited contexts, for the purpose of attaining particular results. This specificity of approach emerges most clearly from the taxation cases,[28] which have been described as *sui generis* and might arguably be regarded as simple exercises in statutory construction.[29] Even beyond this limited category, however, it could be argued that the mere fact that a court "borrows" specific characteristics from the proprietary model in order to rationalise certain aspects of information does not mean that the latter is wholly assimilated in the former.[30]

Secondly, some decisions adopt a proprietary analysis in order to reach a conclusion which may now be attainable without any such analysis. One example may be the *Exchange Telegraph* case,[31] where the grant of an injunction was thought to be dependent upon the plaintiff's establishing some right of property in the subject matter. Another may be the *Yates Circuit Foil* case,[32] which has been described as unnecessarily importing proprietary concepts which were unexceptionably evolved as a means of rationalising certain aspects of the doctrine of restraint of trade into the conditions for an action for breach of confidence.[33]

Thirdly, there is authority to the contrary. It is true that much

27. *Ibid.*
28. E.g., *Rolls-Royce Ltd.* v. *Jeffrey*, above.
29. *Cf.* Stuckey, *op. cit.*, 413.
30. For example, Gurry, *op. cit.*, at pp. 52–53, points out that those cases which adopt the proprietary terminology seem to employ it in two distinct senses: as a metaphor for the contractual and equitable rights which may exist in confidential information, and as an independent jurisdiction, free-standing from both contract and equity. An example of the former usage might be Goff J.'s reference in *Butler* v. *Board of Trade* [1971] Ch. 680 at p. 691, to the confider's "limited proprietary right in equity to restrain a breach of confidence".
31. Above.
32. Above.
33. Stuckey, *op. cit.* at p. 412.

of this, like the authority in favour, deals with the proprietary analysis only in specific contexts. Nevertheless, it is strong enough to demand attention.

AUTHORITY REJECTING A PROPRIETARY ANALYSIS

In *North & South Trust* v. *Berkeley*[34] the plaintiffs had argued that certain information belonging to them had been wrongfully acquired by brokers while acting in the plaintiffs' service. Donaldson J. rejected the argument on the ground, *inter alia*, that it was "by no means clear that information is property in this context".[35] In *Boardman* v. *Phipps*[36] Lord Upjohn dissented strongly from the notion that information was property: "... it is not property in any normal sense but Equity will restrain its transmission to another if in breach of a confidential relationship." In *Fraser* v. *Evans*[37] Lord Denning M.R. remarked that the court's jurisdiction to restrain the publication of confidential information was based "not so much on property or on contract as on the duty to be of good faith".[38] In *Federal Commissioner of Taxation* v. *United Aircraft Corporation*[39] Latham C.J. said:

> "It was argued that the American company transferred to the Australian company information to be used by that company in Australia for a minimum period of five years. It was said that this amounted to a transfer of property—kind of bailment for five years. I am unable to regard the communication of information as constituting a transfer of property. Upon such a communication the transferor still has everything that he had before and the transferee continues to have what he has received even though the five year period has elapsed ...

34. [1971] 1 All E.R. 980; and see *Nichrotherm Electrical Co. Ltd.* v. *Percy* [1957] R.P.C. 207 at p. 209, *per* Lord Evershed M.R.

35. *Ibid.* at p. 993.

36. Above, at pp. 127–128; see also Lord Cohen of Birkenhead at pp. 102–103.

37. [1969] 1 Q.B. 349 at p. 361; cited with approval in *Forster* v. *Mountford & Rigby* (1977) 14 A.L.R. 71 at p. 75, *per* Muirhead J., and in *Wheatley* v. *Bell* [1982] 2 N.S.W.L.R. 544 at p. 550, *per* Helsham C.J. in Eq.

38. *Cf. Gartside* v. *Outram* (1857) 26 L.J. Ch. 113.

39. (1943–1944) 68 C.L.R. 525, 534–535, Aust H.C.; see also *E.I. Du Pont de Nemours Powder Co.* v. *Masland* (1917) 244 U.S. 100, at p. 102, *per* Holmes J. *Commissioner of Taxation* v. *Sherritt Gordon Mines Ltd.* (1977) 51 A.L.J.R. 772, at p. 778, *per* Jacobs J.; *Smorgan* v. *Federal Commissioner of Taxation* (1977) 51 A.L.J.R. 137 at p. 141, *per* Stephen J.

Knowledge is valuable, but knowledge is neither real nor personal property. A man with a richly stored mind is not for that reason a man of property ... It is only in a loose metaphorical sense that any knowledge as such can be said to be property."[40]

A similar aversion to the classification of information as property emerges from English criminal law. It is true that, where information is stored in tangible form (such as on a card or disc) its destruction or damage has been held to be criminal damage.[41] But information *per se* has been held not to be property for the purposes of section 4 of the Theft Act 1968.[42] *Oxford* v. *Moss* concerned an examination paper, to which a student gained unauthorised access; but it has also been regarded as settling, as a matter of principle, that trade secrets cannot be stolen.[43]

Consistently with this, a full equation between information and property has been denied by many academic commentators. The views of Stuckey have already been noted.[44] Goff and Jones[45] state that "information is not, in our view, property,

40. *Cf.*, however, Williams J. (1943–1944) 68 C.L.R. 525, at pp. 547–548, and authorities cited therein: "These considerations all show that, although the rights arise out of contractual or fiduciary relations between individuals, the consequences which flow from that relationship both with respect to the parties to the contract and third parties are such that they may fairly be described, if not in a technical sense, at least in a business sense, as proprietary rights."

41. *Cox* v. *Riley* [1986] Crim. L.R. 460, and *cf. Roger Bullivant* v. *Ellis* [1987] I.C.R. 464 at pp. 474–475, *per* Nourse L.J.

42. *Oxford* v. *Moss* (1978) 68 Crim. App. Rep. 183. *Cf. R.* v. *Morrison* (1859) Bell 158 (pawn ticket can be the subject of larceny).

43. It is interesting to observe, however, that a contrary conclusion has been reached in Canada: see *R.* v. *Stewart* (1984) 149 D.L.R. (3d) 583, discussed by Hammond (1986) 100 L.Q.R. 252 and Weinreb *op. cit.*, and *cf. Attorney-General of Hong Kong* v. *Nai-Keung* [1987] 1 W.L.R. 1339. Moreover, in *Union Carbide Corp.* v. *Naturin Ltd.* [1987] F.S.R. 538 at p. 547, Slade L.J. said: "I am not yet persuaded that a plaintiff *whose confidential know-how has been stolen and used by the thief* to manufacture a product would necessarily be left without rights and remedies, at least against a third party who was in possession of the product and at all material times had full knowledge of all the circumstances in which the product had come into existence" (italics supplied); see also, for a similar use of the language of theft, *Industrial Furnaces Ltd.* v. *Reaves* [1970] R.P.C. 605 at p. 627, *per* Graham J. But Slade L.J.'s remarks were made without any direct analysis of the question of theft, and *Oxford* v. *Moss* was not cited.

44. Above, at p. 88–89.

45. *Law of Restitution* (3rd ed.), p. 653.

at least not in the sense that receipt imposes a duty of enquiry on a third party". Finn[46] describes the concept of property as "a very slippery one in this context", while Cornish[47] points to the lack of firm authority granting the supposed proprietor distinct rights of action against direct interlopers and third party acquirers.

THE COMMERCIAL SIGNIFICANCE OF A PROPRIETARY ANALYSIS

Considerations such as those postulated by Cornish provoke, of course, the crucial question as to how far any proprietary analysis actually enhances our private law of information. Does it genuinely enable the courts to devise coherent and authentic obligations, defences or remedies which might be otherwise unavailable to the parties, or is it simply a frill? There are, it is submitted, a number of respects in which the proprietary analysis might be legally significant, but not all of them are justified by authority.

Priorities, *bona fide* acquisitions and the *nemo dat* rule

In theory, the recognition that valuable information is property might enable that information or its proceeds, or damages for its misapplication, to be recovered from third parties. If the proprietary interest in question were legal, such recovery could be likened to the process whereby an original owner of goods sues a *bona fide* purchaser for conversion under the principle *nemo dat quot non habet*. Admittedly, it might be rare for the information itself to survive in pristine form, undiluted by memorisation on the part of the current possessor or by prior dissemination to third parties: to that extent, a simple repossessory remedy would be of strictly limited value. But if actions for the misuse or adverse detention of informational property were to be treated as comparable to ordinary actions in conversion, several possibilities might arise.

For example, an extension of the analogy into the realm of

46. *Equity and Commercial Relationships*, p. 144.
47. *Intellectual Property* (2nd ed.), pp. 231–233, 240.

available remedies might persuade a court to award against the third party acquirer not merely damages calculated according to the measure awardable in an ordinary case of conversion[48] but some other remedy evolved by comparison with the specific restitution of chattels. Such an alternative remedy might take the form of an order for the delivery up of the information, or of some document or other tangible artefact recording it or arising from it[49]; or the form of an injunction restraining its continued misuse.[50] If such remedies are awardable in actions between the confider and the original recipient of the information, an analysis in terms of legal property might suggest that they should be no less available, in principle, against a third party acquirer. Moreover, it might also be legitimate to apply to actions for the misapplication or adverse detention of informational property an analogy with the doctrine of waiver of tort. This extension of the analogy would enable the original proprietor of the information to renounce his claim for damages or for specific restitution, in favour of the profits of the notional conversion.[51]

Of course, the assumption that information can be the subject of legal ownership raises important consequential issues. For example, if the basic *nemo dat* rule were applicable by analogy to information, should the courts then evolve common law versions of the statutory exceptions to that rule[52] to protect the third party? Without them, the proprietary analogy would be a very blunt instrument; on the other hand, their synthesis would require an almost preposterous ingenuity and boldness.

The more fundamental question is whether an analysis in terms of legal property is doctrinally justifiable at all. Perhaps surprisingly, there are several decisions which appear to accept

48. As were awarded against the original entrustees of the information in *Seager* v. *Copydex (No. 2)* [1969] 1 W.L.R. 809; see below, p. 100.

49. As was awarded against the immediate entrustee of a chattel, from which information was derived in the form of a written report, in *McAlpine & Son Ltd.* v. *Minimax Ltd.* [1970] 1 Lloyd's Rep. 397, discussed by Palmer, *op. cit.*, Chapter 3; and see Stuckey, *op. cit.* at pp. 426 *et seq.*

50. As is advocated by Stuckey, *op. cit.*, pp. 421 *et seq.*, in relation to actions between entruster and entrustee.

51. *Cf. Borden Chemical Co. (Canada) Ltd.* v. *J.G. Beukers Ltd.* (1973) 29 D.L.R. (3d) 337 (bailment of customer list); below, p. 101.

52. Ss. 21–25, Sale of Goods Act 1979; s. 2, Factors Act 1889.

that there may be a "common law" property in information, and thus (by implication) that informational property is not an exclusively equitable phenomenon.[53] One of these authorities is *Deta Nominees Pty. Ltd.* v. *Viscount Plastics Pty. Ltd.*[54] where, admittedly, Fullagar J. went on to conclude that the instant plaintiffs' rights in the ideas which they had communicated to the defendants were property "in the eyes of equity".[55] The second is *Exchange Telegraph* v. *Howard*,[56] where Buckley J. said:

> "The knowledge of a fact which is unknown to many people may be the property of a person in that others will pay the person who knows it for information as to that fact. In unpublished matter there is *at common law a right of property*, or there may be in the circumstances of the case. The plaintiffs here sue, not in copyright at all, but in respect of that common law right of information which they had collected and which they were in a position to sell."

It is tempting to construe the phrase "common law ... right of property" as contemplating a form of legal ownership in information capable of surviving any later disposition to third party acquirers, irrespective of whether they acquired innocently or not and for value or as volunteers. The case for succumbing to this temptation may be especially strong where the proprietor of the information has been divested of his property by some direct incursion or misappropriation on the part of an intermediate recipient, rather than having consensually entrusted the

53. See, for example, *Prince Albert* v. *Strange* (1849) De G. & Sm. 652, 696, *per* Knight-Bruce V.-C.; (1849) 1 Mac. & G. 25, at pp. 42–43, *per* Lord Cottenham L.C.; and see *Wyatt* v. *Wilson* (1820), unreported, cited by Gurry, *op. cit.*, p. 55. This assumption is implicit in decisions which rationalise the recipient's possession of confidential information as the product of a trust, thereby presumably acknowledging a division between legal and equitable property.

54. [1979] V.R. 167, at pp. 190–193, *per* Fullagar J.: "It must ... be borne ... in mind that equity acts *in personam* upon the defendant, that it is only unconscionable conduct that equity will restrain or visit with its other remedies, and that equity only extends any remedy at all where it is satisfied both that it is just in all the circumstances to extend it and that there are no remedies available at common law (e.g., by reason of *property at common law* or of some common law contract) which are in all the circumstances adequate". (Italics supplied.)

55. *Ibid.* at p. 194.

56. (1906) 22 T.L.R. 375; supported by Gurry, *op. cit.*, p. 51. But *cf.* Ashburner, *Principles of Equity* (2nd ed.), at pp. 372–375; Kearney, *The Action for Breach of Confidence in Australia*, at pp. 32–33.

information to him.[57] But in cases, at least, where the third party's acquisition was preceded by a voluntary entrustment by the proprietor to the original recipient, such an interpretation seems at variance with later authority. Even those decisions which apply a proprietary analysis to the disputed acquisition of third party rights in information generally recognise that a *bona fide* purchaser for value without notice will be protected,[58] at least in the period between his original acquisition and his discovery of the proprietor's interest.[59] Such a principle seems consistent only with the distribution of legal property to the original recipient and the retention of a mere equitable property by the claimant. If, however, the only form of property which was capable of subsisting in favour of the proprietor of the information were an equitable property, one might expect that the title purportedly alienated to the third party would be of the same nature, in which event title among competing innocents would presumably be determined by the general rule of priority among conflicting equities, *qui prior est tempore potior est jure*.[60] If, on the other hand, the original property were legal, questions of notice and purchase for value would be immaterial; the original property would subsist unimpaired throughout.

In fact, so far as an entrustment of confidential information has been recognised as capable of constituting a conveyance of property at all, such a conveyance is more typically rationalised in terms of a trust (involving a distribution of equitable

57. *Cf.*, on the facts, *Franklin* v. *Giddins* [1978] Qd. S.R. 78; *Union Carbide Corp.* v. *Naturin Ltd.* [1987] F.S.R. 538

58. E.g. *Morison* v. *Moat* (1851) 9 Hare 241 at pp. 263–264, *per* Turner V.-C.; *Printers and Finishers Ltd.* v. *Holloway* [1965] R.P.R. 239 at p. 253, *per* Cross J.; *International Tools Ltd* v. *Kolar* (1968) 67 D.L.R. (3d) 386 at p. 392, *per* Kelly J.A.

59. *Cf. Stevenson, Jordan & Harrison Ltd.* v. *MacDonald & Evans* (1951) 68 R.P.C. 190; (1952) 69 R.P.C. 10; *Wheatley* v. *Bell* [1982] 2 N.S.W.L.R. 544; *Malone* v. *Commissioner of Police of the Metropolis* [1979] 2 All E.R. 620 at p. 634.

60. It is true that "mere equities" are vulnerable to the purchase of an equitable interest without notice of the prior equity: *Phillips* v. *Phillips* (1862) 4 De G.F. & J. 208 at p. 215; Hanbury and Maudsley, *Modern Equity* (13th ed.), p. 871. But it is questionable whether this analysis offers a constructive explanation of the position of a proprietor of information who seeks to vindicate his title against a third party acquirer: *cf.* Neave and Weinberg (1979) Univ. of Tas. L.R. 24, 115; Hanbury and Maudsley, *op. cit.*, p. 870.

and legal property between entruster and entrustee respectively) than in terms of a bailment (involving a distribution of legal ownership and possession).[61] It would follow that if the information were wrongfully disclosed to, or violated by, a third party, the entruster himself would have no more than an equitable property on which to ground his proprietary claim. Given the recent expressions of antipathy towards actions in tort on the part of equitable proprietors who neither enjoy the immediate right to possession of the property nor have taken the precaution of joining the legal owner as a party,[62] this consideration alone may constitute a formidable bar to any viable proprietary remedy against the third party acquirer. But recent authority has gone further, and has denied that notions of equitable property in information constitute, in any event, a legitimate vehicle for the enforcement of obligations of confidentiality against third party acquirers. In *Wheatley* v. *Bell*,[63] Helsham C.J. in Eq. phrased the rejection in the following terms:

"I am satisfied that the analogy which has been drawn in some of the American cases and by some of the text writers, of the situation of the innocent defendants to *a bona fide* purchaser for value without notice, is not the correct way of approaching the question of whether the injunction should go in the present circumstances or not. The defence of *bona fide* purchaser for value is an equitable defence directed towards the resolution of priorities in relation to property rights. It is an attempt to sort out amongst the claimants interested in property the order in which their various interests should prevail. But I believe that there are no property rights associated with the type of equity involved here; it is an equity to restrain a person from acting in breach of confidence which is owed to another, arising from all the circumstances, and I believe that this is the way in which the authorities, to which I should pay a great regard, have treated the matter. Thus the learned author of *Equity and the Law of Trusts*, Professor Pettit,

61. See, e.g., the quotation by Fullagar J. in the *Deta Nominees* case [1979] V.R. 167 at pp. 191–192 (above, p. 94) and further at p. 194: "... all the information concerning the configuration and mode of manufacture of the drawer of the present case, was in the eyes of equity the property of the plaintiff company."

62. *Leigh & Sillivan Ltd.* v. *Aliakmon Shipping Co. Ltd., The Aliakmon* [1986] A.C. 785 at p. 812, *per* Lord Brandon of Oakbrook; *Parker-Tweedale* v. *Dunbar Bank*, *Financial Times*, 20 December 1989 (C.A.).

63. [1982] 2 N.S.W.L.R. 544 at pp. 549–550.

in the 3rd. ed. (1974) deals directly with this situation ... at p. 422, which reads: 'In any case it is clear that an injunction can be obtained not only against the original guilty party, but against any third party who knowingly obtained the confidential information in breach of confidence or in any other fraudulent manner. Indeed, even if a man obtains the confidential information innocently, once he gets to know that it was originally given in confidence, he can be restrained from breaking the confidence.'"

This refusal to rationalise a claimant's interest in terms of equitable property could, in fact, carry both advantages and disadvantages for third parties. A strict proprietary analysis would suggest that, once the third party has originally acquired the property with the sufficient degree of innocence, no subsequent awareness on his part of the confidential nature of the information can detract from the property he has thus acquired[64]; such a proposition is unlikely to commend itself to modern courts.[65] On the other hand, it is possible that the degree of knowledge which is required in order to subordinate the third party to some pre-existing equitable property in confidential information is less exacting than that required to render him answerable as a participant in a breach of the original recipient's equitable obligation.[66]

An intermediate question, assuming for the moment that information may constitute a form of equitable property, is whether a *bona fide* purchase (for value and without notice) of the legal interest in the tangible record or document containing the information will extinguish any prior equity in the pure information itself. If the tangible and intangible constituents are to be regarded as essentially inseparable for the purposes of the

64. Further, such a purchaser would be entitled to pass a title free from the equitable interest to a successive alienee, even though that alienee had notice of the equitable interest: *Wilkes* v. *Spooner* [1911] 2 K.B. 473. I am grateful to my colleague Mr W. J. Swadling for drawing my attention to this point.

65. Cornish, *op. cit.*, p. 232.

66. See, for example, the judgment of Jacobs P. in *DPC Estates Pty. Ltd.* v. *Grey and Consul Development Pty. Ltd.* [1974] 1 N.S.W.L.R. 433 at

law of criminal damage,[67] it may be legitimate to equate them for this purpose as well. Such conclusions could, however, work injustice to the owner of the information, and must be matched against Lord Radcliffe's acknowledgement in *Rolls-Royce Ltd.* v. *Jeffrey*[68] that informational property is not merely *sui generis* but juridically distinguishable from the records containing it: one can produce a hundred copies of the latter, but one still does not multiply the asset itself.

It is in the context of priorities that one's misgivings about the value of a proprietary analysis of information reach the most disquieting proportions. There is a gaucheness and an artificiality about the analysis (not to mention a capacity for inconvenience) which argues strongly for its abandonment.[69] The

pp. 459, 460, who maintained that in the latter case the claimant must prove that the third party had actual knowledge of the original recipient's breach, "either through knowing or purposely refraining from finding out"; there is no duty of inquiry "to make sure that the fiduciary is not engaging in some dishonest or fraudulent design . . .". In the former case, however: "The confidential information is itself property, and if a person receives that property with knowledge actual or constructive that it is confidential information then he will be liable for profits made by him through the use of that information." In the event, however, Jacobs P. took the view that this case could not be decided on a proprietary basis because it was not clear that the information was either confidential or actually "put to use" by the third party, and because this was not the issue on which the claim had been fought; *cf.* Hutley J.A. at pp. 469–472: "It cannot be suggested . . . that the Walton Group did not lose anything when the information and assistance which caused it to lose its chance to buy the . . . properties were given. What it lost was not property but was analogous to property". On the appeal to the Australian High Court (1975) 132 C.L.R. 373, the views of the majority were somewhat at variance (*cf.* Barwick C.J. and Stephen J. at p. 412 and Gibbs J., who did not find it necessary to decide the issue, at p. 398), but the decision is generally consistent with a refusal to introduce a developed doctrine of constructive notice into this area of fiduciary obligation. For analysis of this difficult question, which is beyond the confines of the present discussion, see Jones, "Restitution of Benefits Obtained in Breach of Another's Confidence" (1970) 86 L.Q.R. 463; Jacobs, *Law of Trusts in Australia* (1977), para. 1321; Stuckey, "The Liability of Innocent Third Parties Implicated in Another's Breach of Confidence" (1981) 4 *University of New South Wales Law Journal* 73, esp. at pp. 80 *et seq.*

67. *Cf.*, for example, *Cox* v. *Riley*, above.

68. [1962] 1 All E.R. 801 at p. 805 *et seq.*

69. Analysis in terms of proprietary principles is conspicuously absent, for example, from the *Guardian* case (above); indeed, at p. 659 Lord Goff of

complexity of its implications suggests that sufficient (if not superior) protection for confidential information already exists within the general law of confidentiality, without resort to theories of property in information. Certainly the Law Commission[70] saw little attraction in importing into this area either common law or equitable principles of priority among competing innocents:

> "... those principles are unsuited to the purpose of resolving the problems relating to the rights and obligations of third parties in the field of information. In the first place, although it is true that in certain cases the owner of property may transfer his rights in it and yet remain in possession thereafter (for example, by constituting himself a trustee for another), such cases do not represent the usual situation where property is transferred. A person may, on the other hand, commonly impart information to others and continue to be in possession of it, concurrently with those others. Furthermore, the present law of confidence has developed along lines different from the principle governing the transfer of property rights and it would clearly be inappropriate for us to introduce the latter principles into a field of law to which hitherto they have not been applied by the courts."

Bailments of information

What, then, of the more limited proposition that, as between entruster and entrustee, the entrustment of information for a specific purpose might fruitfully be approached as akin to a transaction in personalty?[70a] Several judges have favoured an analogy between the entrustment of confidential information and the principles of bailment and conversion. It is true that in *Federal Commissioner of Taxation* v. *United Aircraft Corporation*[71] (where an American company made technical informa-

Chieveley expressly renounced any examination of the "fundamental question" as to whether confidential information may be regarded as property; *cf.*, however, at p. 664, where he observed that consideration of this element in confidentiality cases was an important factor in seeing such problems "in the round".

70. Report No. 110, 1981, p. 9.

70a. The facts of *Forster* v. *Mountford & Rigby* (1977) 14 A.L.R. 71 arguably afford the strongest imaginable example of a case which could be approached as a bailment of information (entrustee living with Aboriginal tribe and being entrusted by them with secrets, the disclosure of which was believed by them to operate inimically to their religion).

71. (1943–1944) 68 C.L.R. 525 at p. 534.

tion available to an Australian company for use over a five-year period) Latham C.J. was unimpressed by the argument that "this amounted to a transfer of property—a kind of bailment for five years." But this was principally because Latham C.J. rejected the notion that information could be property, rather than because he rejected the specific analysis of the transaction. In *Seager* v. *Copydex (No. 2)*,[72] on the other hand, Lord Denning M.R. directly equated the measure of damages payable for a misuse of confidential information with the measure of damages in conversion, producing the result (in his view) that the payment of damages vested the ownership of the information in the defendant.[73] Stuckey,[74] while contending that the award of damages should properly be expressed as a function of the inherent compensatory jurisdiction of Equity, and that the remedial analogy with the chattel torts should be more fully developed to encompass situations closer to claims for specific restitution than to claims for damages in conversion, has welcomed Lord Denning's analogy as "essentially sound in principle and useful in practice." In *Hospital Products Ltd.* v. *United States Surgical Corporation*[75] Mason J. opted squarely for the notion of a bailment of goodwill, the discovery of which could render enforceable obligations comparable to obligations of confidentiality among commercial parties; but his was a dissenting judgment. An earlier English case[76] appears to recruit something akin to the bailment concept as a means of protecting secrets in a master/servant context (although, in fact, a servant does not conventionally become the bailee of his master's property because he does not get possession).[77] In the *North and South Trust* case[78] Donaldson J. seems to accept the bailment analogy, remarking that "the property was never acquired by [the brokers] but was merely in their custody"; but here, as we have seen,[79] Donaldson

72. [1969] 1 W.L.R. 809.
73. It is submitted that later reservations about Lord Denning's approach in *Seager* do not extend to this aspect of the decision: see *Dowson* v. *Mason and Potter* [1986] 1 W.L.R. 1419; *cf*. Cornish, *op. cit*., 232.
74. (1981) 9 Syd L.R. 402, at pp. 417 *et seq*.
75. [1985] L.R.C. (Comm) 411, 458, 461.
76. *Gartside* v. *Outram* (1857) 26 L.J. Ch. 113.
77. Palmer, *op. cit*., Chapter 7.
78. [1971] 1 All E.R. 980 at p. 993.
79. Above, p. 90.

J. had reservations about a proprietary analysis in any event. It is, nevertheless, interesting to contrast the results obtainable upon a bailment analogy with those which would be reached upon the more conventional analysis of a trust or other fiduciary relationship: compare, for example, the hypothetical case of the corporate lawyer discussed by Fullagar J. in *Deta Nominees v. Viscount Plastics*[80] with the defendants' misapplication of a customer list which McKay J. remedied by reference to the tort of conversion in *Borden Chemical Co. (Canada) Ltd. v. J.G. Beukers Ltd.*[81] In the former case, Fullagar J. said:

> "Thus information given for a particular purpose only is, if it is made within the analogy of property of the donor, treated in equity as having been given to the donee upon trust for the purpose only and, subject thereto, held by the donee upon a resulting trust for the donor. When a corporation tells its lawyer that it wants legal advice because it has, unbeknown to the world at large, discovered huge deposits of crude oil in a particular place 180 miles from shore, and that it does not know and seeks to be advised to what government it should apply for licences and so on, that information is given only for the purpose of enabling the advice to be given. If the lawyer were to use that information for other purposes, e.g. to enrich himself by buying a large parcel of shares with the idea of re-selling at a profit when the good news reaches the market, the lawyer would plainly have committed a breach of trust, and he would be forced by equity to account to the donor company whose property the information was, because of the trusts on which the lawyer took the information ... All the cases of so-called trade secrets are examples of this division of property analogy cases."

The comparison is, of course, strengthened by the repeated recognition that a bailee by way of safekeeping occupies a fiduciary position towards his bailor.[82]

The bailment authorities are not strong, and their flimsiness is accentuated by the common belief among authors that

80. [1979] V.R. 167 190 at p. 192; but note the criticism of Meagher, Gummow and Lehane, *Equity: Doctrines and Remedies* (2nd ed.), pp. 822, 834, apparently accepted by Gurry, *op. cit.*, p. 51.

81. (1973) 29 D.L.R. (3d) 337; see Palmer, *op. cit.*, Chapter 3. In this case (arguably on covert principles of the waiver of tort) the court awarded to the bailors the amount of the bailees' profit. An analysis in this vein may, of course, be especially helpful where (as in *Borden*) the claimant is unable (either through financial inability to exploit the information, or from some other cause) to prove any personal loss.

82. E.g. the *Hospital Products* case, above; see generally Palmer, *op. cit.*, Chapter 2.

acceptable results are attainable without resort to fictions drawn from the law of chattels.[83] On the other hand, such analogies may save the courts from "re-inventing the wheel" whenever they are confronted by a novel issue in the law of confidentiality, and are worthwhile even if they do no more than suggest fruitful avenues of exploration. Certainly, a court which wished to introduce the notion of waiver of tort into the misuse of confidential information (thereby enabling the claimant to recover the profits of the misuse) might well find it helpful to approach the entrustment of the information as something akin to a bailment, and its misuse as therefore akin to a conversion of personalty (the traditional tort in respect of which waiver was permitted) rather than to attempt to extend the doctrine outright to a relatively novel and underdeveloped tort of breach of confidence. Admittedly, a constructive trusteeship of the information would often produce similar results. The court might prefer, however, an analysis which conformed with the continued location of *legal* rather than purely equitable property in the confider; and it is not difficult to envisage other reasons for favouring a solution based on waiver of tort, rather than one based on trust.

A further question which might usefully be considered is whether the common law estoppel applicable to conventional bailees (prohibiting them from denying the title of their bailors and from pleading the *jus tertii*) or the common law right of action conferred upon conventional bailees (enabling them to recover full damages from a third party interloper, and precluding that third party from pleading the title of the true owner) should be applied by analogy to the entrustment of information. There may well be advantages in recruiting similar principles to elucidate entrustments of information, and in extending the comparison to the point of recognising that the bailee has an insurable interest in the data. The emerging notion that software might constitute goods for certain purposes[84] clearly strengthens the arguments in favour of bringing other forms of intangible data within the realm of personal property law.

Further avenues of development are also suggested by the

83. Finn, *Fiduciary Obligations*, 131.
84. Below, p. 103.

bailment comparison. It has long been uncertain, for example, whether liability can arise in the absence of contract for a negligent (as against a deliberate) disclosure of information which the discloser knows to be confidential.[85] If the discloser can be treated as a constructive bailee, there is no difficulty in imposing both a duty of reasonable care upon him and the burden of proving that sufficient care has been taken.

Software as goods

A further, somewhat narrower question is whether software can qualify as goods for the purposes of legislation affecting personal property transactions. It seems reasonably clear that pure information does not count as goods within the meaning, for example, of the Sale of Goods Act 1979[86] or the Torts (Interference with Goods) Act 1977. But in *Toby Constructions Products Pty. Ltd.* v. *Computer Bar (Sales) Pty. Ltd.*[87] Rogers J. held that software could, when combined with hardware, constitute goods for the purposes of the implied terms as to fitness and quality contained in the New South Wales Sale of Goods legislation,[88] and he left open the question whether such an identity could be enjoyed by the software alone.[89] Developments in North America suggest that software will, in time, be classified as goods by the English courts[90] and that a software licensing agreement might, for example, qualify as something akin to a contract for the hire of goods for the purposes of sections 6–10 of the Supply of Goods and Services Act 1982.

Likewise, in the case of the Torts (Interference with Goods)

85. Law Commission Report No. 110, 1981, pp. 26–27.
86. See Benjamin, *Sale of Goods* (3rd ed.), 63.
87. [1983] 2 N.S.W.L.R. 48.
88. A recent unreported English decision seems to proceed on a similar assumption, but the point was not argued: *Mackenzie Patten & Co.* v. *British Olivetti Ltd.* (1984) unreported, 11 January. *Cf. Cox* v. *Riley*, above.
89. [1983] 2 N.S.W.L.R. 684, at p. 691. But *cf.*, denying the possibility of a bailment of, or property in, spoken words or mechanically transmitted messages, *Primrose* v. *Western Union Telegraph Co.* (1893) 154 U.S. 1, esp. at pp. 14–15; *Malone* v. *Commissioner of Police of the Metropolis* [1979] 2 All E.R. 620 at p. 630, *per* Megarry V.-C.
90. See, for example, Andrew Rodau, "Computer Software: Does Article 2 of the Uniform Commercial Code Apply?" in (1986) 35 *Emory Law Journal* 853; James H. Salter, "Software Performance Standards under Article 2 of the Uniform Commercial Code" in (1989) 9 *Computer Law Journal* 465.

Act 1977, an adventurous court might wish to adapt the remedies afforded under the Act to situations involving the misuse of software or other data. We have already seen that, in *Seager* v. *Copydex (No. 2)*,[91] Lord Denning M.R. reached a conclusion about the proprietary effect of a judgment in damages for breach of confidentiality which was closely comparable to the principle now acknowledged by section 5 of the 1977 Act. The liberal use of analogies derived from section 6 of that Act (which deals with the "innocent improver" of goods) might help to solve the problems caused when an originally unknowing purchaser for value of confidential information discovers its confidential nature only after he has made a substantial outlay in improving it, or in preparing to exploit it.

CRITERIA FOR A PROPRIETARY ANALYSIS

Cornish[92] suggests three specific tests for establishing the proprietary quality of confidential information. He maintains that such information will acquire the characteristics of property only when rights are given against third parties in the circumstances outlined by him. The tests are: (i) does possession of the information in private *per se* generate rights against those who misappropriate it? (ii) if know-how is assigned, does the assignee acquire the assignor's rights to sue both direct and indirect recipients who are breaking the confidence? and (iii) in the case of two licences or assignments to different parties by way of inconsistent dealings, does one of them attain priority over the other, and if so on what principle? On the latter point, Cornish cites *De Beer* v. *Graham*[93] (where it was held that neither recipient had more than a personal right against his source) as tending to negate the proprietary quality of information. He points out, however,[94] that under modern law an undertaking that the provider of the information will not dispose of it to anyone else may generate an obligation of confidence binding on a later recipient.

91. Above.
92. *Op. cit.*, p. 240.
93. (1891) 12 L.R.N.S.W. Eq. 144.
94. *Op. cit.*, p. 240, fn. 78.

Austin[95] is more critical of the categorisation of information as property, and advances four reasons against it. First, he contends that such an approach gives no guidance as to the direction the law should take; ridiculous results would ensue if all information were treated as property, but it is difficult to separate those categories which should be so treated from those which should not. Secondly, he argues that it can produce wrong results: a volunteer receiving from a fiduciary would be liable as a constructive trustee, whereas a *bona fide* purchaser of the information for value would not be. Thirdly, it would prevent trustees or other fiduciaries from disclosing information even if they resolved unanimously to do so in the best interests of their beneficiaries or principals, for if information is property its disclosure would necessarily amount to a wrongful disposal thereof. (This would also create great problems for professional trustees.) Fourthly, it would make for inflexibility of remedies, because strictly speaking no allowance could be made to account for the fiduciary's skill or effort in turning the information into gain.

These assertions are not beyond question. In relation to the second, for example, it may still be legitimate (at least in special cases) to recognise a common law property in information, producing the reservation of a legal interest in favour of the claimant; such characterisation would render immaterial questions of notice and purchase for value. Austin's fourth criticism arguably describes the precise sort of situation in which adaptation from the law of personal property would be desirable, and in which analogies based (for example) on the doctrines of accession and improvement have a beneficial function. Such comparisons might be derived from statute (see section 6 of the Torts (Interference with Goods) Act 1977) or even from the law of real property, arriving via the law of personalty (as, for instance, with the notion of proprietary estoppel).

CONCLUSION

At the very least, Austin's analysis reminds us of the need to conduct future classifications of information more sensitively

95. *Constructive Trusts* in Finn, *Essays in Equity*, pp. 223 *et seq.*

and selectively, and with a sharper awareness of the limitations of juridical labels, than has hitherto been the case. It is unacceptable merely to attach the property label as an afterthought, in a decision which is amply justifiable by reference to some other analysis (such as the discovery of a fiduciary relationship between the parties). It is equally unacceptable to impose some unnecessarily universal characterisation upon a particular category of information, purely to attain a desired result in a single case.

Certainly, there is a risk that a proprietary analysis of information may produce a less refined set of responses than solutions drawn candidly from the emergent (and still malleable) law of confidentiality alone. But the problems here may not be insuperable. For example, it seems difficult at first sight to understand how the property analysis might accommodate a public interest defence. But an answer of sorts had been evolved as far back as *Gartside* v. *Outram*,[96] with Turner V.-C.'s assertion that there could be no property in an iniquitous or fraudulent subject matter.[97] Again, it is not immediately apparent why informational property should be limited to information which is confidential. But in *Deta Nominees Pty. Ltd.* v. *Viscount Plastics Pty. Ltd.*[98] Fullagar J. had no hesitation in stating a common-sense test as to whether information was property, based upon the expectations of the reasonable person:

"Would a person of ordinary intelligence, in all the circumstances of the case, including, *inter alia*, the relationship of the parties and the nature of the information and the circumstances of its communication, recognise this information to be the property of the other person and not his own to do as he likes with."

96. Above.

97. Admittedly, however, the issues of public interest and freedom of information present a formidable challenge to the judicial development of any proprietary analysis of information. As Kearney, *op. cit.*, at pp. 33–34 remarks, the question of public interest in disclosure is difficult "because there are real questions of conflicting interests and conflicting social policy. That is, the policy that confidences should not be divulged against the policy of free speech and free flow of information. These are not solved by giving one party property rights and thus a broad power to restrict disclosure ... This has the potential to be most inequitable."

98. [1979] V.R. 167 at p. 193; and see further at pp. 191, 194. See also *Searle & Co. Ltd.* v. *Celltech Ltd.* [1982] F.S.R. 92 at p. 105, where it was remarked that the plaintiffs had "a proprietary interest in information ... provided that ... the information was acquired ... in circumstances which imposed ... in equity an obligation of confidence"; Gurry, *op. cit.*, pp. 52–53.

The property analysis is not, therefore, without its resources. But one cannot overstate the need for a complete awareness of its implications before pursuing each application to its final conclusion. Former judicial classifications of information as property have arguably done as much to obscure the essential questions of policy and principle at issue as to elucidate them; future tribunals may be better advised to confront specific issues directly and individually, without invoking all-purpose solutions of marginal conceptual value. But in confronting the particular issues, the courts should remain alive to the value of analogy; for as Gurry[99] has remarked, although the status of the property analysis remains uncertain, its confirmation would have the desirable effect of providing the courts with a valuable additional jurisdiction by which confidential information could be protected. Only then can the courts effectively address Finn's description of the proprietary controversy as "Perhaps the most sterile of the debates which have arisen around the subject of information received in confidence",[100] and mount a decisive endeavour to comprehend issues of confidentiality "in the round".[101] *

NORMAN PALMER

99. *Op. cit.*, p. 55.

100. *Fiduciary Obligations*, p. 131.

101. *Attorney-General* v. *Guardian Newspapers Ltd. (No. 2)* [1988] 3 All E.R. 545 at p. 664, *per* Lord Goff of Chieveley.

* The author thanks Joanna Goyder, Research Co-Ordinator, Baker & McKenzie, for valuable research assistance.

CHAPTER 6

CONFIDENTIALITY AND LABOUR LAW

From the point of view of the labour lawyer, confidentiality is interesting because the duties imposed by law upon an employee to respect confidential information acquired in the course of his job can be explained in different ways. On one view, the employee's duty is to be explained by reference to a term, express or implied, in the contract of employment; on another the duty is seen as resting on the nature of the relationship within which the information is imparted. Strictly speaking, there is no conflict between these two explanations: contractual and equitable duties co-exist and overlap here, just as in other areas (such as the obligation to provide safe systems of work) contractual and tortious obligations may operate in tandem.[1] For many purposes the "great conceptual confusion"[2] concerning the true nature of confidentiality is irrelevant, though it clearly is not when it comes to the question of specific remedies, the improper use of confidential information by third parties, and the economic torts.

When an employee is induced to divulge confidential information by a third party, this will amount to inducement to break

1. But note the views of Lord Greene M.R. in *Vokes Ltd.* v. *Heather* (1945) 62 R.P.C. 135, 141–142, to the effect that it was unhelpful to consider "equitable" as opposed to "contractual" confidentiality in the context of the employer/employee relationship. This opinion has not been followed; see Law Commission No. 110, *Breach of Confidence*, 1981, p. 18, fn. 85. See also A. Stewart, "Confidentiality and the Employment Relationship" (1988) 1 *Australian Journal of Labour Law* 1–22.

2. G. Jones, "Restitution of Benefits obtained in Breach of Another's Confidence" (1970) 86 L.Q.R. 463.

a contract, and will generally be tortious.[3] There are also special features of the contractual duty. It will often survive the ending of the contract of employment itself, and there is no contradiction in talking of the post-employment duties in respect of confidentiality as governed by contractual principles in the same way as duties arising while the contract is extant.

As a generalisation, the attention of the labour lawyer tends to concentrate on the contractual side of confidentiality, and this article follows that approach. We shall consider the interrelationship between the duty of confidentiality and other terms of the contract of employment. A full discussion of the different remedies following on breach of confidence is left to the equity lawyers, but one particular remedy of a very recent origin—the so-called "garden leave" cases—ties in with the law relating to covenants in restraint of trade, and is discussed below. Finally, the question of confidentiality in relation to the law of unfair dismissal is briefly considered.

Within the "contractual" framework two themes predominate: confidentiality in relation to the implied terms of the contract, and confidentiality in relation to covenants in restraint of trade. A covenant in restraint of trade may be incorporated within a contract of employment, or it may take the form of an additional and separate agreement, collateral to that contract.

CONFIDENTIALITY AND IMPLIED TERMS

Although commonly spoken of as an independent obligation, the actual duty to respect confidentiality is really best seen as a particular obligation of the duty of fidelity. Just as the employee is not permitted to make private profits for himself instead of for his employer, or undertake activities which place him in competition with his employer (even where, in some cases, such activities take place out of working hours,[4] so also he is bound to respect confidentiality. The implied duty of fidelity is moreover a crucial one, in the sense that breach of it will, subject to the observance of any relevant disciplinary procedures, typi-

3. *Brents Brewery Co. Ltd.* v. *Hogan* [1945] 2 All E.R. 570; *Norbrook Laboratories Ltd.* v. *King* [1984] I.R.L.R. 200, N.I.C.A.

4. *Hivac Ltd.* v. *Park Royal Scientific Instruments Ltd.* [1946] Ch. 169.

cally justify the response of summary dismissal; in other words breach of the duty of fidelity will amount to "gross misconduct" by the employee.

Sometimes the question whether or not information is confidential (in the sense of capable of being protected by the employer) will get mixed up with the question whether the way it was acquired was permitted by law. To take an example, the employee who writes down or memorises a list of his employer's customers while he is employed, with a view to approaching them subsequently to do business with him when he has left employment, is one of the clearest examples of breach of the duty of fidelity.[5] The breach of contract lies in the act of deliberately writing down names for such an improper purpose. It is better to describe the wrong in this way than to assert that the list of customers is confidential information—something which is very difficult to maintain in the light of the leading authority of *Faccenda*.[6] In that case it was held that sales information, including lists of customers and prices, did not qualify as confidential information for the purposes of being subject to a restriction after employment had ended. Thus, breaches of contract may well result from behaviour that leads to the disclosure of information which is not, *per se*, properly regarded as capable of protection. The content of the duty of fidelity (the duty of good faith) will vary according to the nature of the contract—a point particularly mentioned in *Faccenda*.[7] It will also vary according to the nature of the work done—it is easier, for example, to imply a term that working for a competitor out of hours is in breach of the duty of fidelity if the employee is of managerial status.[8]

CATEGORIES OF CONFIDENTIALITY IN EMPLOYMENT

In the light of the above, and following the guidance given in *Faccenda* itself, we can classify the information which an

5. *Wessex Dairies Ltd.* v. *Smith* [1935] 2 K.B. 80, C.A.
6. *Faccenda Chicken* v. *Fowler* [1986] 1 All E.R. 617, C.A.
7. *Per* Neill L.J. at p. 625. *Cf. Sim* v. *Rotherham Metropolitan Borough Council* [1986] I.C.R. 897, E.A.T., another example of where the implied terms of the contract were significantly dependent on the professional nature of the engagement.
8. *Hivac* v. *Park Royal Scientific Intruments Ltd., supra*, fn. 4.

employee acquires in the course of employment into four main categories:

1. Information which is a "trade secret" in the fullest sense. Secret formulae, and design processes are the clearest examples of this type of information, but it is capable of extending to other highly confidential matters as well.[9] Disclosure or improper use of such information is forbidden both during the contract and after it has ended. This is clearly "confidential" information and attracts the strongest protection under law; for this reason it is henceforth described here as a "grade 1 secret". This category excludes, however, confidential information that can be described as business know-how—that is, information which is acquired as a necessary skill as part of the job. (See category 3 below.)

2. Information which it would be breach of contract for the employee to disclose during the currency of the contract of employment, but which may be disclosed or used once the contract has ended. Here the information is not "confidential" in any strong sense of that word, but disclosure during employment will nevertheless constitute a breach of the duty of fidelity. An example might be information about the company's trading position or financial state—something which could be discovered by an outsider, but only by close scrutiny and analysis of published accounts. This is the category which seems to be covered by the dictum in *Faccenda* referring to "information which is only confidential in the sense that an unauthorised disclosure to a third party while the employment subsisted would be clear breach of the duty of good faith." In *Norbrook Laboratories* v. *King*[10] disclosure of details relating to financial grants received from a public authority was treated as a breach of contract, though the information could have been discovered by an outsider taking a certain amount of trouble.

3. Information which is "confidential" in the sense that it forms part of the employee's "know-how" in the job. This category includes not only the kind of information which has to be acquired if the job is to be done properly, but also information relevant to manufacturing processes which, though perhaps not capable of being seen as a "grade 1 secret", cannot be separated

9. *Herbert Morris Ltd.* v. *Saxelby* [1916] 1 A.C. 688.
10. [1984] I.R.L.R. 200, N.I.C.A.

from the employee's general stock of knowledge inevitably acquired in doing his job.[11] An example of "know-how" that is unprotected is given by *Faccenda* itself—the knowledge of customers and their preferences that is inevitably available to a sales manager. While such confidential information may not be disclosed during the currency of the contract, there is no restriction to its disclosure or use after the ending of the contract. In *Roger Bullivant* v. *Ellis*[12] a card index containing lists of trade customers was described as information falling within this category. (The decision also shows how deliberate and unlawful use of such information during employment will amount to a breach of the duty of fidelity.)

4. Information which does not fall into any of the above categories and may be regarded as being in the public domain. No breach of fidelity occurs when this is disclosed to third parties, even when the contractual relationship is in being.

In practice, it is the distinction between information in categories 1, 2 and 3 which gives rise to most problems in situations where there is no express term relating to confidentiality in the contract.

Faccenda gives us guidance as to how we should try to differentiate between categories 1 and 3 in circumstances where there are no express terms in the contract about confidentiality. We are told that several considerations are relevant:

- what is the nature of the employment? If the employment necessitates the habitual handling of "grade 1 secrets", then there is likely to be a high degree of confidentiality imposed on employees—i.e. this makes it more likely that information will be subject to post-employment disclosure or use of information will be prohibited.
- what is the nature of the information itself? The information must be either a grade 1 secret or is at least material which is akin to it because it is highly confidential in nature, if it is to be subject to post-employment restrictions.
- whether the employer impressed on the employee the

11. *Printers & Finishers Ltd.* v. *Holloway* [1964] 3 All E.R. 731, C.A.
12. [1987] I.R.L.R. 491, C.A.

confidentiality of the information in question. If he did, this is a factor in favour of post-employment restrictions on its use.

— whether the relevant information can be easily isolated from other information which the employee is free to use or disclose. The more easily separable it is from information which is not protected, the easier it is to argue that it is subject to post-employment control.

Labour lawyers are familiar with this kind of approach as a means of resolving difficult decisions. Essentially, the same approach is used as a means of settling the age-old dilemma of whether an individual is employed or self-employed.[13] Its attraction for the judiciary is that it gives the appearance of certainty, while in fact making it almost impossible to challenge on appeal the judgment of the court or tribunal called upon to make the classification. It should also be pointed out that if an employer wishes to seek an injunction to restrain a breach of the duty of confidentiality, it is incumbent upon him to define the breach clearly. Failure to make it clear to the ex-employee what it is he must not do will strongly militate against the granting of an injunction.[14]

One particular situation which deserves special mention in the context of remedies arises when an injunction is sought to restrain the use or disclosure of confidential information in circumstances where there is a strong public interest attaching to such disclosure. In effect, the courts have fashioned an exception to the general rules restricting an employee (or ex-employee's) duties towards his employer, on the basis that the duty owed to the public will take precedence over any contractual or equitable limitation. A recent decision[15] illustrates the point clearly. Following a dispute over payment between an employee formerly engaged as a compliance officer by a financial services company, the employee indicated an intention to disclose certain information about the company's operations to the regulatory body (FIMBRA) with responsibility for overseeing the proper functioning of such firms. In proceedings concerned with the

13. *Ready Mixed Concrete (South East) Ltd.* v. *Minister of Pensions and National Insurance* [1968] 2 Q.B. 497, Q.B.D.

14. *Lawrence David Ltd.* v. *Ashton* [1989] I.R.L.R. 22, C.A.

15. *Re a Company's Application* [1989] 2 All E.R. 248, Ch. D.

continuation of an injunction prohibiting such disclosure, Scott J. took the view that there should be no prohibition against the disclosure of confidential information to official regulatory bodies (or the Inland Revenue), even in the event of the employee's behaviour being actuated by malice. Going beyond the facts of the case itself, it is interesting to speculate to what extent this ruling might apply to other types of whistle-blowing. In particular, the disclosure of confidential material about working systems in circumstances where there was a perceived danger to health and safety should probably receive similar treatment, provided disclosure was to the proper body (Health and Safety Executive).

CONFIDENTIALITY AND COVENANTS IN RESTRAINT OF TRADE

As we have established above, information which is confidential but also part of "business know-how" will not be the subject of post-employment restrictions on use and disclosure by reason of any implied term within the contract. Should an employer wish, however, to improve his position in law, he may (and often will) seek to extend his rights by using a restrictive covenant. In *Faccenda* an important part of the judgment lies in the Court of Appeal's expressed opinion that if an employer sought to make use of this technique, he would succeed only in so far as the resulting restrictive covenant satisfied the general qualifications imposed by law on such undertakings.

On the other hand, there is nothing to prevent an employer from increasing the duties owed by the employee within the contract of employment. The company's rules may make disclosure of any information a disciplinary matter. Should an employee be in breach of the rules, this will amount to a breach of the contract of employment on his part, and the fact of being in breach of the rules will be an important—though not decisive—consideration should a claim for unfair dismissal ensue. So an employer can give himself additional protection over the use of information through the (disciplinary) terms of the contract of employment which he will draw up and usually be able to insist on as part of the contract. The breach of a purely disciplinary rule will not lead on to the special remedies associated with the bringing of an action in equity for breach of confidence; a simple breach of company rules will not give a remedy against third parties.

Where such protection is desired, the necessary device available to an employer is that of a restrictive covenant. The standard rules here are well known: any such covenant must be seen as entered into for the protection of legitimate interests of the employer, and that it must be shown by the employer to impose limits that are no more than reasonably necessary to give such protection. The legitimate interests that may be furthered are the protection of trade secrets category 1 in the classification given above and the solicitation of customers.

"An employer is entitled to take and enforce promises from an employee which the employer can prove are reasonably necessary to protect him, the employer, his trade connection, trade interests and goodwill, not from competition by the employee if he leaves his employment, or from him then using the skill or knowledge with which his employment had equipped him to compete, but from his then using his personal knowledge of his employer's customers or his personal influences over them, or his knowledge of his employer's trade secrets, or advantages acquired from his employment, to his employer's disadvantage."[16]

The Court of Appeal made it clear in *Faccenda*, differing from the view taken in the court below, that the employer may not use a restrictive covenant to protect non-confidential information (i.e. falling within categories 2, 3 or 4 above). This is so even though the disclosure or use of such information during the currency of the contract would constitute a significant breach of the implied duty of fidelity or some express disciplinary rule of the undertaking. Any direct attempt to prolong such obligations after employment has ended will be permissible only in so far as the strict standards relating to the purpose and content of restrictive covenants are met. It may, however, be possible to achieve indirectly the employer's objective by curtailing through the obtaining of injunctive relief the taking up of employment by the ex-employee in certain limited circumstances. This possibility is considered below. But, first, one point

16. *Spafax Ltd.* v. *Harrison* [1980] I.R.L.R. 442, C.A., 446, *per* Stephenson L.J.

may be made about a basis on which a particular covenant may be challenged as invalid because of the circumstances in which the employer seeks to rely upon it.

CHALLENGING RESTRICTIVE COVENANTS

This is not the place to consider all the many rules governing the challenging of restrictive covenants by reference to their contents. But a recent decision[17] of the Court of Appeal signals an interesting development relating to challenge by reference to the employer's conduct. The background is the fundamental rule that an employer may not rely on an otherwise valid restrictive covenant in circumstances where he has himself repudiated the terms of the contract.[18] When will such repudiation take place? The easy example is where the employee is summarily dismissed in circumstances where it is ruled that he did not commit gross misconduct. The employer's refusal to give notice where in law this is due is just one example of repudiatory conduct. But there are many other possibilities. The *Parker* decision re-opens an old question: does the employer repudiate the contract when he terminates by paying wages in lieu of notice? The terms of the contract there provided that the contract might be determined "by the giving in writing of six calendar months' notice on either side or the payment of six months' salary in lieu thereof". This was construed as allowing two lawful ways of termination by the employer, so that the enforceability of the restrictive covenant could not be challenged on this ground by the employee. The Court of Appeal reached this conclusion, however, only after distinguishing an earlier decision[19] in which Sir John Donaldson had indicated that payment of wages in lieu was to be seen as payment of damages for breach of contract by the employer. The basis for the distinction made in *Parker* was the wording of the particular contract, which was said to

17. *Rex Stewart Jeffries Parker Ginsberg Ltd.* v. *Parker* [1988] I.R.L.R. 483, C.A.

18. *General Billposting Co.* v. *Atkinson* [1909] A.C. 118.

19. *Dixon* v. *Stenor Ltd.* [1973] I.R.L.R. 28, N.I.R.C. In *Gothard* v. *Mirror Group Newspapers* [1988] I.R.L.R. 396, C.A., Sir John Donaldson M.R. expressly refused to overrule his earlier statement, although he did insist that it be interpreted in the context in which it was made.

be a "material and critical difference". Arguably, where the contract only provides for termination by notice, without the option of payment of wages in lieu—a phenomenon by no means unusual—the employer who dismisses with wages in lieu may be unable to enforce an otherwise valid restrictive covenant against an employee who has gone.[20] One way of testing the situation is to look at what might happen if the situation were reversed. Can an employee, required by contract to give notice of termination, avoid being in breach if he leaves without notice, but offers to pay to the employer a sum of money equivalent to the wages he would have earned had he worked out his notice? It is thought not, since presumably the employee's services must be worth more to the employer than the wages paid, otherwise there would be no advantage to the employer in the existence of the relationship. There is no direct authority on this question, but there is a fair amount of authority on the issue of whether the employer who dismisses with wages in lieu is in breach,[21] including one decision[22] supporting the view that the answer will depend on the construction of the particular contract. With respect, this would seem to be the right approach. From the practical point of view, it would seem a wise precaution, in any context in which a restrictive covenant is relevant, for an employer to make provision for the break clause in the contract to cover payment by wages in lieu as well as by the giving of notice.

The nature of payments in lieu of notice is important in other areas of law too. It may, for example, affect the availability of remedies under the Wages Act. It has been held, albeit only at the level of an industrial tribunal,[23] that even if pay in lieu of notice is properly categorised as damages for breach of contract, an employee may still use the Wages Act 1986 to recover such sums unlawfully withheld.

There is another way in which a restrictive covenant might

20. Against this view, there is the dictum of Mr John Mowbray, Q.C., in *Spencer* v. *Marchington* [1988] I.R.L.R. 393, that, "if an ordinary minor employee at a wage is told not to work out a month's notice on dismissal, I should be very surprised if that involved a repudiation".

21. See, e.g., M.R. Freedland, *The Contract of Employment*, Oxford, 1976, pp. 181–185.

22. *White* v. *Riley* [1921] 1 Ch. 1.

23. *Jackson* v. *Foster Wheeler (London) Ltd.* [1989] I.R.L.R. 283, I.T.

be challenged by reference to an employer's conduct, although it is not one that so far has been the subject of litigation. Let us assume a termination with notice has taken place. Often this will be because the employer is dissatisfied with some aspect of the employee's behaviour. If the contract includes a disciplinary procedure and the terms of that procedure are capable of applying to the unsatisfactory behaviour of the employee, will it be a repudiatory breach of contract if the disciplinary procedure is not followed? The recent decision in *Dietman* v. *London Borough of Brent*[24] draws attention to the contractual significance of disciplinary procedures, and to the importance of close scrutiny of their wording. There is no contradiction in law in saying that an employee who has committed an act of serious misconduct is still, by the tems of his contractually-incorporated disciplinary procedure, entitled to a hearing or other safeguard before being dismissed. If the employer should neglect to observe such standards, then in principle he should, under the *General Billposting* authority, be precluded from relying on an otherwise valid covenant in restraint of trade. On the other hand, there is no reason why the terms of employment should not include, alongside the contractually incorporated disciplinary procedure, a provision expressly retaining the employer's right to terminate the contract by the giving of notice, or wages in lieu, and again the inclusion of such a provision might be a wise precaution for an employer to take in the drawing up of his contractual documents.

THE "GARDEN LEAVE" CASES

In the last few years the traditional reluctance of the courts to grant injunctions to enforce terms within the contract of employment has altered. Both from the point of view of the employer and the employee, the obtaining of injunctive relief has become significantly easier[25] in specific situations. An employer, faced with an employee who is apparently leaving

24. [1988] I.R.L.R. 299, C.A.

25. The details of the changes from the employee's point of view fall outside this article; see, e.g., H. Carty, "Dismissed Employees: the Search for a More Effective Range of Remedies" (1989) 52 M.L.R. 449.

his job in breach of contract to work for a competitor, may be able to restrain such action for the unexpired portion of the contract by obtaining an injunction from the court.[26] In this way the employer may in effect be able to protect himself for a time against the employee's exploitation of information and knowledge acquired in the course of his employment—even in the absence of any covenant in restraint of trade. The main condition will be that the employer offers to pay salary during the period in question (hence "garden leave"), with the result that the employee is not faced with either having to starve or perform the terms of the contract, a situation which is unacceptable to the courts because it is seen as amounting to specific performance of the contract.[27] This new development of the law is of considerable importance for companies which employ high-status executives on fixed-term contracts. But it is a development subject to important limitations. In particular, the longer the period for which such an injunction is sought, the greater the difficulties for the ex-employer in obtaining it. And, as a recent decision[28] makes clear, a court will in any event be reluctant to grant such relief in the absence of evidence that the employer seeking it will suffer detriment by the ex-employee's proposed move.

CONFIDENTIALITY AND UNFAIR DISMISSAL

The last point to consider is whether a dismissal of an employee for improperly disclosing or making use of information will provide the basis for an employer fairly dismissing him or her. No categorical answer is possible, since much will depend on the circumstances of the disclosure and the information misused. The general principles of unfair dismissal law will of course apply, so the question whether the employer is seen as having acted reasonably will certainly be influenced by whether or not the employer had observed fair procedures in taking action.[29]

In the context of unfair dismissal it is best to view confidentiality as one aspect of the general and wider duty of fidelity owed by an employee.

26. *Evening Standard Co. Ltd.* v. *Henderson* [1987] I.R.L.R. 64, C.A.
27. *Warner Bros. Pictures Inc.* v. *Nelson* [1937] 1 K.B. 209, C.A.
28. *Provident Financial Group plc* v. *Hayward* [1989] I.R.L.R. 84, C.A.
29. *Polkey* v. *A.E. Dayton Services* [1987] I.R.L.R. 503, H.L.

The duty of fidelity will not give an employer the right to dismiss fairly a manual employee who is working in his spare time for a competitor.[30] Here the courts seem inclined to follow the approach of the common law, as expounded in *Hivac*.[31] Similarly it will not be fair to dismiss someone just because they have the intention of going to work for a competitor.[32] A recent decision[33] takes this approach one stage further. An employee used his knowledge of his employer's suppliers, gained as part of his job as warehouse manager, in order to write letters to them asking for product lists, price lists and terms. He was dismissed summarily by his employer, and this dismissal was held unfair. Although his purpose in writing the letters was to gain information that would enable him to set up in business in competition, he had broken no term of his contract by what he did. It might have been different, said the court, if he had been engaged in such action during working hours, or if the intended competition was going to take the form of behaviour in breach of an enforceable duty relating to confidentiality. Presumably, it would also be significant if the terms of the contract had contained a valid restrictive covenant restraining the employee from undertaking the business activities which he had in mind.

Where an employer fears that an employee will in the future disclose information, then this can amount to some other substantial reason for dismissal, and such a dismissal may well be fair. But it will be necessary to take into account the degree of access the employee enjoys to confidential information, the importance of such information and the position held by the employee.[34] In such a situation, however, the manner in which the dismissal is implemented will again be important.

BRIAN NAPIER

30. *Nova Plastics Ltd.* v. *Frogatt* [1982] I.R.L.R. 146, E.A.T.
31. *Supra*, fn. 4.
32. *Harris and Russell Ltd.* v. *Slingsby* [1973] I.R.L.R. 69, N.I.R.C.
33. *Laughton* v. *Bapp Industrial Supplies Ltd.* [1988] I.R.L.R. 245, E.A.T.
34. *Skyrail Oceanic Ltd.* v. *Coleman* [1980] I.R.L.R. 226, E.A.T.

CHAPTER 7

WHAT CONFIDENCE IN COMPUTER MISUSE?

Before the end of the 1990 parliamentary session, barring unforeseeable political earthquakes, the law of England and Wales will have made for the first time statutory provision "...for securing computer material against unauthorised access or modification". That provision, as expressed in the long title to the Computer Misuse Bill,[1] will have implications for the confidentiality of information but is not based on any explicit development of the law relating to breach of confidence. The purpose of this essay is to look at those implications and to highlight the need in this context to extend civil remedies for breach of confidence along the lines recommended by the Law Commission in its 1981 Report.[2] First, however, it is necessary to look at the background to the 1990 Bill, the relevant provisions of the 1990 Bill, and the current law relating to breach of confidence and information acquired by improper means.

BACKGROUND TO THE 1990 BILL

The Computer Misuse Bill is based on two documents produced by the Law Commission: Working Paper No. 110, *Computer Misuse*,[3] and Report No. 186, also entitled *Computer Misuse*.[4] The former document took the form of a "green paper"

1. All references in this Chapter to the Computer Misuse Bill are to House of Commons Bill 115, as amended in Standing Committee C in proceedings on the 14, 21 and 28 March 1990.
2. Report on *Breach of Confidence*, Law Com. No. 110, Cmnd. 8388, (1981).
3. Issued in September 1988; hereafter "Working Paper".
4. October 1989, Cn. 819; hereafter "Report".

discussion document. The latter, produced after extensive consultation, contained the Commission's recommendations which, with only minor alterations, were enshrined by parliamentary counsel in the 1990 Bill.

Although the Law Commission's final report was accelerated in order to be ready for the 1989–1990 parliamentary session, it was not, after an initially warm government welcome, awarded the status of a programme Bill. Instead the responsible department, the Department for Trade and Industry, gave support—both tacit by not blocking the Bill in Parliament and active in terms of drafting and other legal assistance—to a Private Member's Bill introduced by Michael Colvin, M.P.[5] This method of enacting the Law Commission's recommendations was less than ideal, because of the limited parliamentary time available for debate and the consequent difficulty in amending the Bill in any substantial respect. However, the continuing assistance of the Law Commission throughout the Bill's passage helped to ensure a continuity of policy.

It is only possible to understand the scope of the Computer Misuse Bill by looking at the task the Law Commission set out to accomplish. In the Working Paper the Commission first described a range of activities which might be categorised as "computer misuse",[6] and then considered how far such activities were already or ought to be covered by the criminal law. Its provisional conclusion was that, with few exceptions, the criminal law dealt satisfactorily with those areas of computer misuse identified. The law either excluded such conduct as insufficiently serious to warrant criminal sanctions (as with for example, the unauthorised use of office computer facilities for personal word-processing), or included such conduct within the ambit of general offences relating to theft, fraud and criminal damage. The "broad band" nature of offences under the Theft Act 1968 and the Criminal Damage Act 1971 and the wide scope of common law conspiracy to defraud persuaded the Commission at that

5. Mr Colvin's Bill enjoyed all-party support. The Bill's other sponsors were Sir Geoffrey Pattie, John Butcher, Kenneth Warren, Michael Grylls, Emma Nicholson, William Powell, Tam Dalyell, Norman Hogg, Terry Davis, Doug Hoyle and Matthew Taylor.

6. A neutral term consciously chosen in preference to the (racier!) "computer crime": see Working Paper, para. 1.5.

stage that there was no need for a comprehensive code of computer-specific offences in English law. Any reform, it was suggested, should be directed to the plugging of those gaps which were identified.[7]

For present purposes, the only relevant lacunae identified by the Law Commission related first, to that behaviour commonly described as "hacking" and, secondly, to "eavesdropping" on a computer.

Computer hacking

The conduct in question

For Working Paper purposes hacking meant "the obtaining of unauthorised access to a computer".[8] What was implied by that definition was not physically walking into a computer room, but using, typically, a micro-computer and "modem" in order to access a target computer system through the public telecommunications system. The password which will let the hacker into the computer system will either be known to him or will be found by trial and error, perhaps using a program which rapidly generates many permutations of letters and numbers.

The Law Commission concluded that the criminal law did not extend to the mere obtaining of unauthorised access to a computer by hacking, except perhaps to a limited extent in respect of dishonestly abstracting electricity[9] and under the Data Protection Act 1984.[10]

In particular, the Law Commission noted that the unauthorised use of someone else's password to gain access to a computer did not amount to forgery. That point was forthrightly decided by the Court of Appeal and the House of Lords in *R.* v *Gold*

7. See Working Paper, paras. 8.1–8.10. Appendix to the Working Paper contained a survey of other jurisdictions' attempts to grapple with computers.
8. *Ibid.*, para. 2.10.
9. Contrary to section 13 of the Theft Act 1968. See *ibid.*, paras. 3.23–3.25.
10. Any criminal sanction under the Data Protection Act probably exists only in theory: it is difficult to envisage the Data Protection Registrar undertaking a prosecution based on the holding of personal data without being registered as a data user (contrary to section 5 of the 1984 Act) in all but the most extraordinary case of hacking. The Commission's analysis of the relevant law is to be found at *ibid.*, paras 3.49–3.60. See also J.A.L. Sterling, *The Data Protection Act 1984* (2nd ed., 1985), para. 690.

and Schifreen.[11] The defendants had been convicted of several counts of forgery[12] in 1986 at Southwark Crown Court after they had gained access to British Telecom's "Prestel" electronic mail system and, in particular, to the Duke of Edinburgh's personal (empty) mailbox, using passwords that they were not entitled to use.[13] Subsequently, in July 1987, their convictions were set aside by the Court of Appeal, a decision later confirmed by the House of Lords. Both appellate courts rejected as artificial the Crown's contention that that part of the computer in which the password was held while it was checked against known passwords ("the user segment") could be regarded as a "false instrument" within the 1981 Act. Having reached that conclusion, Lord Brandon added that:

"...I share the view of the Court of Appeal (Criminal Division), as expressed by Lord Lane C.J., that there is no reason to regret the failure of what he aptly described as the Procrustean attempt to force the facts of the present case into the language of an Act not designed to fit them."[14]

The robust rejection of hacking as forgery by the English courts gave rise to the obvious question of what mischief unauthorised access to a computer actually caused. From the Law Commission's analysis, two approaches can be discerned. First, hacking might threaten the confidentiality or privacy of information.[15] Secondly, hacking might be regarded as a disruptive influence on the computer system itself, irrespective of the information it contains or the functions it carries out.

Hacking and the protection of information

The Law Commission's Working Paper focussed on the need to protect information stored on a computer by drawing atten-

11. [1988] Q.B. 1116 (C.A.); [1988] A.C. 1063 (H.L.).

12. Contrary to section 1 of the Forgery and Counterfeiting Act 1981.

13. It should be pointed out that unauthorised access was achieved by the simple expedient of entering a "1-2-3-4" type sequence followed by a codeword along the lines of "2222222"! The defendants said that one of their motives was to alert Prestel to the lack of security in its system.

14. [1988] A.C. 1063, at p. 1073B.

15. I take confidentiality as referring to an obligation owed by one person to another. Privacy, on the other hand, arises by virtue of the nature of certain kinds of information. See report on *Breach of Confidence*, Law Com. No.110, Cmnd. 8388 (1981), paras. 2.2–2.3.

tion to the computer's enormous information storage and processing ability, the use of computers for holding sensitive information and the security problems inherent in guarding a system which, in order to be effective, has to be accessible from remote locations. Two of the options suggested for discussion as possible frameworks for an extension of the criminal law to cover hacking were formulated in terms of obtaining unauthorised access to information, alternatively to certain limited classes of information, stored on a computer.[16] These options for reform reflected the conclusion of the Scottish Law Commission which recommended in its report on "Computer Crime" that reform of the law of Scotland was necessary in order to create a crime of hacking aimed at the protection of information stored on computers.[17]

The English Law Commission's options for reform were in addition to a "do nothing" option and the Commission expressed no preference for any particular course of action. The intention behind the Working Paper was to obtain reliable evidence about the nature and extent of the risk posed by hacking to computer owners and users and the options put forward were designed to elicit responses on the need to protect computerised information by criminalisation, rather than simply by security measures.[18]

Hacking and the protection of computer systems

The second alternative basis for an extension of the criminal law to cover hacking was what the Law Commission's Report described as[19]: "... the need to protect the integrity and security of computer systems from attacks from unauthorised persons seeking to enter those systems." That need to protect computer systems' integrity was suggested to the Commission on consultation by those concerned that the Working Paper had overemphasised the "information storage" role of computers at the

16. See Working Paper, para. 6.20, for a summary of the options put forward for reform.
17. Scot. Law Com. No. 106, July 1987 at paras. 3.6, 3.13(2) and 3.14(2)–(3).
18. See Working Paper, para. 6.18.
19. Para. 1.37.

expense of their "operational" role. Operational computer systems perform a multitude of functions: for example, they administer financial transactions through systems such as SWIFT—the world-wide inter-bank fund transfer system—and share dealing systems, and they operate stock control mechanisms, travel services, manufacturing processes and payroll procedures. The Commission's Report expresses its conclusion on the hacking evidence obtained during the consultation exercise as follows[20]:

> "... [H]acking by unauthorised entry or attempted entry is sufficiently widespread to be a matter of major and legitimate concern to system users ... The concern about this form of hacking is not so much the possibility of inadvertent damage to the system ... but the uncertainty and cost caused by repeated hacking attempts. This concern has frequently been described to us as concern about the 'integrity' of the system attacked. Put briefly, because of the possibility that any attempted entrant may have had password access to important levels of authority, sometimes to a level which has enabled him to delete records of his activities from the system, any successful unauthorised access must be taken very seriously. Substantial costs are therefore incurred in (i) taking security steps against unauthorised entry and in the equally important precaution of monitoring attempts to enter; and (ii) investigating any case, however trivial, where unauthorised entry does in fact occur."

That passage is of crucial importance in understanding the hacking offences contained in the Computer Misuse Bill. Whereas the Working Paper had adopted a neutral view to the criminalisation of hacking, the consultation exercise persuaded the Law Commission that new criminal offences were necessary for reasons which did not depend primarily on confidentiality. Accordingly it was not necessary for the Commission to attempt to answer the vexed question of whether the criminal law should protect confidentiality or private information merely because that information was stored on a computer. If that had been the only ground for a new criminal offence then the Commission would have had, it said, "difficulty"[21] in recommending its creation. However, in view of the evidence supporting an offence aimed at protecting "computer integrity", the fact that such an offence would in effect increase the protection of computerised

20. Report, para. 1.29.
21. *Ibid.*, para. 2.13.

information was not felt to be a sufficiently strong argument against the creation of the new crime.[22]

Eavesdropping on a computer

The second lacuna in the law identified by the Law Commission's Working Paper was surreptitious surveillance on a computer. Several august bodies have examined this subject in England and Wales alone, among them the Younger Committee, the Phillips Commission and indeed the Law Commission itself.[23] Further, the efforts of Mr Malone in this field[24] led directly to the Interception of Communications Act 1985, section 1(1) of which provides that: "...a person who intentionally intercepts a communication in the course of its transmission by post or by means of a public telecommunication system..." shall be guilty of an offence, triable either way and punishable on conviction on indictment with up to two years' imprisonment. That offence was intended to include the interception of computer data transmitted along telephone lines.[25] However, one of the criticisms of this much-criticised piece of legislation[26] was that it did not regulate the use of electronic listening devices or visual surveillance methods. In particular, the Law Commission took the view that "eavesdropping" on a VDU screen by, for example, monitoring radiation emitted by it in order to reconstruct the legitimate user's screen display on the eavesdropper's own VDU, was outside the scope of the 1985 Act and,

22. *Ibid.*

23. Report of the Younger Committee on Privacy (1972) Cmnd. 5012; Report of the Royal Commission on Criminal Procedure (1981) Cmnd. 8092, paras. 3.53–3.60; Report on Breach of Confidence, Law Com. No. 110, Cmnd. 8388 (1981).

24. Starting with *Malone* v. *Commissioner of Police of the Metropolis (No. 2)* [1979] Ch. 344.

25. See the comments of the Home Secretary in *Hansard*, H.C. (1985) Vol. 76, col. 1135.

26. *The Times*, 6 March 1985 called the Bill an act of "dumb insolence" designed to comply with the bare minimum standards necessary under the European Convention of Human Rights. The *Financial Times*, 8 February 1985 greeted the White Paper preceding the Bill by saying that "...the best advice seems to be to say and write as little as possible." For the background to the Act and the view that it does not necessarily achieve even the limited ambition ascribed to it in *The Times*, see I.J. Lloyd (1986) 49 M.L.R. 86.

therefore, unless the information gained was covered by the Official Secrets legislation, no criminal offence would apply.[27]

The distinction betwen eavesdropping (whether electronically, as described above, or simply by looking at someone else's screen) and hacking is that with the former there is no control over the information accessed and consequently none of the risk of disruption inherent in the latter. No real distinction can be made however between unauthorised surveillance on a computer and unauthorised surveillance in general. Both subjects raise important general principles about privacy and confidentiality. For that reason, in the Working Paper the Commission made it clear that it considered the problem beyond the scope of its exercise and, further, that it was at that stage opposed to the inclusion of such conduct in a hacking offence.[28] The Commission added in its Report that the technical evidence which it had received indicated that, with present technology, electronic eavesdropping on VDU screens was only possible under "... the most favourable conditions and using sophisticated and expensive equipment ...", and therefore in quantitative terms the threat was quite small.[29] By contrast, it is possible to hack using a relatively cheap micro-computer and modem connected to a telephone line.[30]

THE PROVISIONS OF THE COMPUTER MISUSE BILL 1990

The 1990 Bill creates three new criminal offences:

27. Working Paper, para. 3.31.

28. Paras. 3.32 and 6.22. The concern about the overlap of a hacking extent was caused by the use of "obtaining unauthorised access" as the phrase describing hacking. That phrase is capable of including electronic eavesdropping and indeed the Scottish Law Commission saw no objection to that result: Scot. Law Com. No. 106 (1987), para. 4.14.

29. Report, para. 3.25.

30. See the conviction of Nicholas Whiteley, *The Times*, 25 May 1990, for criminal damage. The defendant caused £25,000 damage to computer disks by hacking from his own bedroom into university computer systems using equipment available for about £600 (see also the *Sunday Correspondent*, 27 May 1990).

(1) Unauthorised access to computer material—"the unauthorised access offence".[31]
(2) Unauthorised access with intent to commit or facilitate commission of further offences—"the ulterior intent offence".[32]
(3) Unauthorised modification of computer material—"the modification offence".[33]

In order to assess the implications of these offences for the law relating to breach of confidence it is necessary briefly to outline their scope.

The unauthorised access offence

The essence of this offence is that a person commits it if[34]:

"(a) he causes a computer to perform any function with intent to secure access to any program or data held in any computer;
(b) the access he intends to secure is unauthorised; and
(c) he knows at the time when he causes the computer to perform the function that that is the case."

The intent referred to in (a) need not be an intent to secure access to any particular data or kind of data.[35]

The ulterior intent offence

A person who commits the unauthorised access offence with the additional intent to commit or facilitate the commission of a further offence such as, for example, theft, is guilty of this offence. It extends inchoate liability back in time to include cases where the suspect has embarked on a criminal venture but, having gained unauthorised access, has not yet done an act which is "more than merely preparatory" (within section 1(1) of the Criminal Attempts Act 1981) to a further substantive offence.

31. A summary offence punishable with up to six months' imprisonment or a fine of up to £2,000 or both.
32. An either way offence punishable on conviction on indictment with up to five years' imprisonment.
33. An either way offence punishable on conviction on indictment with up to five years' imprisonment.
34. Clause 1(1) of the Bill.
35. Clause 1(2).

The unauthorised modification offence

For present purposes, it is sufficient to note that this section, broadly speaking, protects data and programs in the same way that the Criminal Damage Act 1971 protects tangible property.[36] It makes the erasure of the contents of a computer's hard disk by electronically "deleting" those contents an offence in the same way that physically throwing the computer out of a fifteenth storey window is already an offence.

BREACH OF CONFIDENCE—A REMEDY FOR HACKING AT PRESENT?

The latest edition of *Clerk & Lindsell on Torts* devotes, for the first time, a whole chapter to the subject of breach of confidence.[37] Under the heading "Information improperly obtained" it is said that[38]:

> "Information may come into a party's hands not by being communicated directly to him but by dishonest means or a trick. The use of information improperly obtained will be restrained even where, for instance, a document might be relevant in legal proceedings. In practice, once such information has been obtained it may pass on from the person who originally obtained it to others, who will likewise be enjoined from making use of it even if they receive it innocently." (Footnotes omitted.)

If that is a correct statement of the law there seems to be no reason why a hacker who dishonestly obtains unauthorised access to confidential information held on a computer should not be restrained from using that information by an action for breach of confidence. For example, if a businessman arranges for a computer expert to hack into a rival's computer system in order to discover his expansion plan over the next five years, can his rival, on finding out about this breach in security, obtain injunctive relief to prevent the use of that information and/or damages?[39] The same result should logically follow if the infor-

36. For the full ambit of the offence and its application to computer "viruses" and "worms" see Report para. 3.65.

37. 16th ed. (1989), Chapter 31.

38. *Ibid.*, para. 31–11(d).

39. Both would be normal remedies for a breach of confidence action: see *Clerk & Lindsell*, paras. 31–17–31–20.

mation had been obtained by the use of an electronic eavesdropping device reconstructing the victim's VDU display. Such an action, including the availability of *ex parte* interlocutory relief, would, one imagines, present a more immediate attraction to the disgruntled victim than reporting the matter to the police and waiting for a prosecution for the new unauthorised access offence.

The main obstacle to an action for breach of confidence as a remedy against information acquired by hacking is the decision of Sir Robert Megarry V.-C. in *Malone* v. *Metropolitan Police Commissioner*.[40] That case concerned the tapping of Mr Malone's telephone by the Post Office at the request of the police (on the authority of the Home Secretary's warrant) and the subsequent use of information so obtained in Mr Malone's trial for handling stolen goods. The Plaintiff sought a declaration to the effect that, *inter alia*, he had a right of confidentiality in respect of telephone conversations on his telephone lines and interceptions were in breach of that right. The Vice-Chancellor stated that, if a case of breach of confidence is to succeed, three elements are required. First, the information itself must have the necessary quality of confidence about it.[41] Secondly, the information must have been imparted "...in circumstances importing an obligation of confidence".[42] Thirdly, there must be an unauthorised use of that information to the detriment of the party communicating it.[43] Whereas in the *Coco* case, the Vice-Chancellor continued, a manufacturer allegedly misused information supplied to him by a designer, the alleged misuse in the *Malone* case was by someone to whom the plaintiff had no intention of communicating anything. Those circumstances introduced what Megarry V.-C. called the new "unknown overhearer" element to the case. In his view[44]:

"...a person who utters confidential information must accept the risk

40. [1979] Ch. 344.
41. *Ibid.*, at p. 375, citing Lord Greene M.R. in *Saltman Engineering Co. Ltd.* v. *Campbell Engineering Co. Ltd.* (1948) 65 R.P.C. 203, 215.
42. *Malone* at p. 375, citing Lord Widgery C.J. in *Coco* v. *A.N. Clark (Engineers) Ltd* [1969] R.P.C. 41, 47.
43. *Ibid.*
44. *Malone* at p. 376.

of any unknown overhearing that is inherent in the circumstances of communication. ... I do not see why someone who has overheard some secret in such a way should be exposed to legal proceedings if he uses or divulges what he has heard. No doubt an honourable man would give some warning when he realises that what he is hearing is not intended for his ears; but I have to concern myself with the law, and not with moral standards. There are, of course, many moral precepts which are not enforceable.

When this is applied to telephone conversations, it appears to me that the speaker is taking such risks of being overheard as are inherent in the system. ... In addition, so much publicity in recent years has been given to instances (real or fictional) of the deliberate tapping of telephones that it is difficult to envisage telephone users who are genuinely unaware of this possibility. No doubt a person who uses a telephone to give confidential information to another may do so in such a way as to impose an obligation of confidence on that other: but I do not see how it could be said that any such obligation is imposed on those who overhear the conversation, whether by means of tapping or otherwise."

Those dicta are very wide and suggest, on one view, that gaining access to information by hacking, while deserving of moral opprobrium, does not amount to circumstances importing an obligation of confidence. Indeed, the Law Commission's report on *Breach of Confidence* concluded, on the basis of *Malone*, that it was very doubtful whether it could properly be said that in acquiring information by reprehensible means the obtainer becomes subject to an obligation of confidence.[45]

Since *Malone* was decided, however, two decisions have suggested the existence of a broader right to restrain the use of improperly obtained information. In *Francome* v. *Mirror Group*,[46] the plaintiffs sought to restrain a newspaper from publishing extracts from tapes of telephone conversations obtained by unauthorised surveillance methods and alleged to show breaches of the rules of horse racing by the first plaintiff, the well-known National Hunt jockey. One defence put forward by the newspaper, appealing against an interlocutory injunction restraining publication, was that *Malone* was authority for the view that there was no cause of action against it or the original eavesdropper for breach of an obligation of confidence. Reject-

45. Law Com. No.110, Cmnd. 8388 (1981), para. 4.10.
46. [1984] 1 W.L.R. 892.

ing this contention as "a rather surprising proposition", Sir John Donaldson M.R. pointed out that in *Malone* the Vice-Chancellor had explicitly confined himself to dealing with telephone tapping authorised by a properly issued warrant, and decided nothing on tapping for other purposes, or by other persons, or by other means.[47] It was not necessary for the court in *Francome* to decide at that stage whether there was a cause of action, but it did say that the point was "a live issue".[48]

The second recent case is *I.T.C. Film Distributors* v. *Video Exchange Ltd.*[49] The facts of the main action are unimportant in this context, because the reported decision turned on an incident which took place after a hearing in court on an interlocutory motion when one of the defendants obtained "by a trick" a box containing the plaintiff's files.[50] Those files included material such as solictor's attendance notes, a joint opinion of counsel and also documents that would not be privileged from discovery in the main action. Warner J. accepted that *Lord Ashburton* v. *Pape*[51] was:

"...not an isolated decision but is illustrative of a general rule that, where A has improperly obtained possession of a document belonging to B, the court will, at the suit of B, order A to return the document to B and to deliver up any copies of it that A has made, and will restrain A from making any use of any such copies or of the information contained in the document."

Lord Ashburton v. *Pape* was a clear case of breach of confidence by a solicitor's clerk in which Swinford Eady L.J. said it was a general principle to restrain the publication of confidential information "improperly or surreptitiously obtained".[52] In *I.T.C.* Warner J. took the view that, had the defendant not already sworn an affidavit exhibiting the "stolen" documents, he would have granted relief along the lines of that granted in *Lord Ashburton*. However, the general rule propounded by Warner J. does not clearly differentiate between breach of

47. *Ibid.*, at p. 895 citing *Malone* at p. 384.
48. *Francome* at p. 895.
49. [1982] Ch. 431.
50. *Ibid.*, at p. 437.
51. [1913] 2 Ch. 469.
52. [1913] 2 Ch. 469 at p. 475.

confidence and a remedy based on copyright in the documents themselves.[53]

It may well be that, at present, the better view is that the businessman victim in the example given above would have a remedy based on breach of confidence.[54] Certainly *Francome* and *I.T.C.* would assist in establishing such a cause of action and, where the motive was dishonest and access clearly unauthorised it would be unattractive, in my view, for a court to decide that the risk of information being extracted from a computer system in this way was a risk "inherent in the circumstances". The Law Commission said in 1981 that[55]: "Any attempt to state the existing law on a field untouched by legislation, and where the decided cases have provided no clear signposts, runs the danger of being rendered out-of-date by an innovating decision." In some areas of law it might of course be desirable and perfectly satisfactory to wait for an innovative decision to establish the matter finally but, I would submit, the considerations in this context are manifestly too complex to be left to the common law on a case by case basis. Should for example the casual or chance eavesdropper be restrained? If not, where should the line be drawn? Furthermore, the Law Commission has already produced recommendations and draft legislation that would deal with the matter comprehensively within a new statutory action for breach of confidence.[56] The Commission's proposals were stimulated by what it saw as the "glaring inade-

53. Statements to similar effect can indeed be supported by dicta in two early copyright cases: *Webb* v. *Rose* (1732) cited (1769) 4 Burr. 2303, 2330; and *Miller* v. *Taylor* (1769) 4 Burr. 2303, 2378–2379. See further Law Com. No. 110 at para. 4.8

54. That view has been taken in the past by, for example, Gareth Jones (1970) 86 L.Q.R. 463, 482 and J. and R. Jacobs (1969) 119 New L.J. 133. For Commonwealth assistance see the Queensland decision of *Franklin* v. *Giddins* [1978] Qd. R. 72 (noted by W.J. Braithwaite in (1979) 95 L.Q.R. 313) where Dunn J. said that: "I find myself quite unable to accept that a thief who steals a trade secret, with the intention of using it in commercial competition with its owner, to the detriment of the latter, and so uses it, is less unconscionable than a traitorous servant" and upheld an action for breach of confidence against a defendant who stole budwood cuttings from a unique strain of nectarine trees in order to develop an orchard to compete with the plaintiff's.

55. Law Com. No. 110, para. 4.8.

56. In Law Com. No. 110, discussed in the section below.

quacy"[57] of the law in this area and, while recent decisions have added to the arguments, they can scarcely be said to have removed all the doubts.

THE 1990 BILL AND THE NEED FOR FURTHER REFORM

Under the 1990 Bill a hacker who obtains unauthorised access to information intending to use that information for his own purposes would be guilty only of the summary unauthorised access offence. It would not be possible to charge him with the aggravated offence of securing unauthorised access with intent to steal because, for the purposes of the Theft Act 1968, information is not property and therefore cannot be stolen.[58]

If an offence of unauthorised access is suspected, the Law Commission explain in their Report that it is technologically perfectly possible to locate the hacker by monitoring the target computer.[59] One amendment to its recommendations, however, is the new power to issue a search warrant given to a magistrate who is satisfied that there are reasonable grounds for believing that an unauthorised access offence is being committed in any premises and evidence thereof is to be found in those premises. That provision, in clause 14 of the Bill, is analogous to the power contained in section 15 of the Wireless Telegraphy Act 1949 to enter and search premises for "pirate radio" equipment. The aim in the latter case is to catch the operator "red-handed" and similar considerations are likely to be present in suspected hacking incidents.

The obvious irony of the 1990 Bill is that, while a hacker may now be prosecuted for the unauthorised access offence, on the law as it stands there is no certainty that he could be restrained from using the information which he obtained. On the other hand, the criminal law has not yet taken up (with

57. *Ibid.*, para. 5.5.

58. *Oxford* v. *Moss* (1978) 68 Cr. App. R. 183. The decision of the Ontario Court of Appeal that confidential information could be stolen was overruled on appeal by the Supreme Court of Canada: *R.* v. *Stewart* (1988) 50 D.L.R. (4th) 1.

59. Report, paras. 2.20–2.23.

the exception of the Interception of Communications Act 1985) the question of eavesdropping.

The Law Commission's Report on Breach of Confidence contained a fully worked out statutory remedy which I shall not attempt to explain in detail. In this context, however, one recommendation is worth citing in full[60]:

"(7) A person should owe an obligation of confidence in respect of information acquired in the following circumstances:

(i) by unauthorised taking, handling or interfering with anything containing the information;
(ii) by unauthorised taking, handling or interfering with anything in which the matter containing the information is for the time being kept;
(iii) by unauthorised use of or interference with a computer or similar device in which data is stored;
(iv) by violence, menace or deception;
(v) while he is in a place where he has no authority to be;
(vi) by a device made or adapted solely or primarily for the purpose of surreptitious surveillance where the user would not without the use of the device have obtained the information;
(vii) by any other device (excluding ordinary spectacles and hearing aids) where he would not without using it have obtained the information, provided that the person from whom the information is obtained was not or ought not reasonably to have been aware of the use of the device and ought not reasonably to have taken precautions to prevent the information being so acquired."

Statutory provision along those lines in the form of a new statutory tort of breach of confidence would have the merit of approaching the problem of confidentiality comprehensively while ensuring that the special security problems of computerised information were properly dealt with in the scheme.

In conclusion, the Law Commission's work and the 1990 Bill has focussed debate on the approach of the criminal law to computer security. The new offences created will increase the protection given by the criminal law to information stored in computer systems. In my view it is unfortunate that the opportunity has not yet been taken to act on the Law Commission's proposals in respect of unauthorised surveillance. During the passage of the Interception of Communications Act 1985 the

60. Recommendation (7) at para. 7.2.

Home Secretary said that the government intended to introduce legislation implementing those recommendations.[61] By 1987, however, the government's position was that legislation was not a high priority because the Report on breach of confidence amounted essentially to a restatement of the common law.[62] In the light of that Report's conclusion that the present law was glaringly inadequate in relation to unauthorised surveillance,[63] that position seems to me to be difficult to sustain.[64]

JEFFREY CHAPMAN

61. *Hansard* (H.C.), 12 March 1985, Vol. 75, col. 157.
62. *Hansard* (H.C.), 2 February 1987, Vol. 109, col. *513* (written answers).
63. At para. 5.5.
64. The author, who worked on the computer misuse project at the Law Commission until publication of its Report, gratefully acknowledges the assistance he derived from all those involved in the exercise, but especially Brian Davenport, Q.C., and Richard Buxton, Q.C., the Law Commissioners with special responsibility for criminal law at the time of the Working Paper and the Report respectively. Naturally no one but the author is responsible either for the views expressed here or for the errors that remain.

CHAPTER 8

FREEDOM OF SPEECH AND PUBLICATION IN THE PUBLIC INTEREST

How successfully do our courts reconcile the proper acknowledgment of the principle of freedom of speech with the imposition of prior restraints upon publication by way of interlocutory injunction? This process of reconciliation is one which is particularly subtle and controversial in the Anglo-Australian courts because no constitutional guarantee of freedom of speech can be invoked and determinations therefore depend wholly upon the interpretation and application of common law principles.

One thing that can clearly be asserted even in relation to those countries in which such a constitutional guarantee exists, is that the freedom is never an absolute one; it is always a qualified, relative one. Even in the U.S. where the First Amendment provides a strong constitutional guarantee of freedom of expression, there have been cases in which prior restraints were upheld.[1] In the *Pentagon Papers* case, the majority refused the injunction in that particular case but agreed that a prior restraint would be upheld to prevent the publication of secret government information in circumstances where: "[I]t will surely result in direct, immediate and irreparable damage to our nation or its people."[2] Six judges agreed with this qualification of the freedom. It is worth noting, however, that two judges, Black and Douglas JJ., reiterated the absolutist view that the First Amendment wholly precludes any prior restraint at all.[3]

1. These cases are discussed at pp. 150–151 *infra*.
2. *New York Times* v. *U.S.* (1971) 403 U.S. 713 at p. 730 (*per* Stuart J.).
3. 403 U.S. 713 at pp. 713–715.

There are many excellent articles dealing with this decision, in particular,

It is commonly held that the traditional common law view of liberties such as the freedom of expression is that such freedoms do not form part of our substantive law. They exist only in so far as they have not been abrogated or restricted either by statute or rules of the common law. On this view, justified on philosophical grounds most notably by Isaiah Berlin's concept of "negative liberty" in his essay "Two Concepts of Liberty",[4] our law has always been conceived of as a catalogue of particular wrongs, our liberties or "rights", being the residue of unprohibited conduct.[5] Even if this were generally true in the times of the ancient forms of action, which this writer doubts, this is certainly no longer generally the case and in particular, no longer the case in relation to the principle of freedom of expression and its subsidiary principle of the freedom of the press. Certainly these principles are ones which are regarded by the Anglo-Australian courts as substantive considerations to be weighed respectively against others in reaching a satisfactory decision on a particular question of prior restraint. As Lord Goff said in the final House of Lords *Spycatcher* decision: "We, in this country, (where everybody is free to do anything, subject to the provisions of the law) proceed rather upon the assumption of freedom of speech and turn to our law to discover the established exceptions to it."[6] In Dworkin's now classic analysis, Ethe concept of freedom of speech is a principle, not a substantive rule. It is a principle, rather, which must be weighed in the formulation of a satisfactory substantive rule in the particular case. This essay addresses itself to the question of consistency: how consistently is the principle acknowledged in the varieties of cases in which an interlocutory injunction to restrain publication has been sought?

And in addressing the issue of consistency, the writer will address two specific, but interrelated, issues:

Henkin L., "The Right to Know and the Duty to Withhold: The Case of the Pentagon Papers" [1971] 120 Uni. Penn. L.R. 271; and Cox A., "Freedom of Expression and the Burger Court" (1980) 94 Harv. L.R. 1.

4. In *Four Essays on Liberty* (London, 1969).

5. See A. Boyle, "Freedom of Expressions as a Public Interest in English Law" [1982] *Public Law* 574 and J.F. Burrows, "The House of Lords and Freedom of the Press" (1982) 3 (No. 3) *Jo. of Media Law and Practice* 278.

6. [1988] 3 W.L.R. 776 at p. 808.

(1) Does a principle analogous to the rule in defamation cases known as the rule in *Bonnard* v. *Perryman*[7]—which forbids the grant of an interlocutory injunction if there is any likelihood that a jury would accept the defendant publisher's plea of justification, qualified privilege or fair comment on a matter of public interest—operate in breach of confidence cases?

(2) Should interlocutory injunctions be granted on an alternative ground (e.g. breach of copyright, passing off or injurious falsehood) in cases where on the same set of facts an injunction would *not* be available either: to restrain a defamation (by virtue of the rule in *Bonnard*[8]); or to restrain a breach of confidence (by virtue of the public interest defence)?

DOES A PRINCIPLE ANALOGOUS TO THE BONNARD v. PERRYMAN RULE OPERATE IN BREACH OF CONFIDENCE CASES?

The relationship between the actions for defamation and breach of confidence seems problematic but on analysis, is ultimately a complementary one. The function of the action in defamation is to protect reputation by ensuring the telling of the truth in the public interest. The function of the action for breach of confidence involves the suppression of the truth for the preservation of other social goods, namely, privacy, trade secrecy and the preservation of confidence in institutional decision-making by maintaining bureaucratic and governmental secrecy.[9] So, the action for breach of confidence can be invoked to prevent the disclosure of true information, never intended for the public domain, provided that the information has been conveyed in the context of the kind of confidential relationship which Equity will protect. The action is a personal action in Equity. What

7. [1891] 2 Ch. 269.
8. *Ibid.*
9. See P.D. Finn, "Confidentiality and the Public Interest" (1984) 58 A.L.J. 497.

one needs to prove is the existence of such a relationship and its breach (or the threat thereof). There is no need to prove detriment. For defamation, what must be proven is the publication of falsity and damage. In breach of confidence, the wrong lies in the publication of secret information even if true; in defamation, the wrong lies in the publication of falsity resulting in provable harm.

It is most interesting that until recently, it was only in the law of defamation that the principle of freedom of speech was recognised as founding a substantive rule of law. The rule is that in *Bonnard* v. *Perryman*[10]—that no interlocutory injunction will be granted if the defendant can show that he will avail himself of any one of the three defences to publication at trial. The defences are justification, qualified privilege or fair comment on a matter of public interest. The mere assertion that the defendant will legitimately plead one of these is usually sufficient: certainly, there will be no injunction if there is any likelihood that the jury would accept the defendant's plea. For an injunction, the court will require that the plaintiff establish that the words are untrue, i.e. that no jury could reasonably find the words to be true, and that damages will not be an adequate recompense for the injury wrought by publication.[11] The exceptional rule created in *Bonnard* v. *Perryman* has survived the leading modern decisions in relation to interlocutory injunctions in general in both Britain and Australia: *American Cyanamid* v. *Ethicon*[12] and *Beecham* v. *Bristol Myers*.[13]

Thus, in defamation cases, prior restraint by way of interlocutory injunction is rarely obtained. The policy basis of the rule in *Bonnard* v. *Perryman*, a case concerning publication by a newspaper, is clearly the principle of freedom of expression and its subsidiary principle, freedom of the press. But what makes these injunctions objectionable is not simply that they are imposed to restrict freedom of expression and may therefore operate to discourage publication permanently when used effec-

10. See fn. 7, *supra*.

11. See J.G. Fleming, *The Law of Torts* (7th ed., Law Book Co.) Chap. 25; R. Pound, "Equitable Relief Against Defamation and Injuries to Personality" (1916) 29 Harv. L.R. 640; and R.A. Hayes, "Injunctions before Judgment in case of Defamation" (1971) 45 A.L.J. 125.

12. [1975] A.C. 396.

13. (1968) 118 C.L.R. 618.

tively as a means of intimidation but that the wrongfulness of the publication is not fully established at the time the injunction is sought. The issue as to whether the words are defamatory has traditionally been a matter for the jury and is a further reason, if now somewhat historical in some jurisdictions, for the reluctance of the courts to grant such injunctions.

It is worth noting in this context that there is also a rule of procedure which enshrines the principle of freedom of the press: the "newspaper rule". In terms of the legal rules, the press have no greater rights than the individual citizen to publish but the role of the press as voluntary agent of the public's right to know is recognised in this rule of procedure which provides that interrogatories aimed at discovering the source of a libel are not allowed in libel proceedings against newspapers at the interlocutory stage. The reason for this rule of procedure is that the plaintiff is assured of his damages in the action against the newspaper and needs no second defendant at that stage. Of course, the principle underpinning this procedural rule must be that of freedom of the press. In recent years the press have sought unsuccessfully to elevate this procedural rule to the status of an absolute immunity protecting confidential press sources from disclosure at any stage of the proceedings. This attempt has been rebuffed in both the U.K. and Australia: *BSC* v. *Granada*, House of Lords[14]; *John Fairfax* v. *Cojuangco*, Australian High Court.[15]

So, the basic judicial practice is against prior restraint in defamation cases. How does that situation compare with breach of confidence cases where the critical remedy is prior restraint—because the preservation of secrecy is all, because there are doctrinal and jurisdictional problems in providing adequate remedy if the injunction is not granted or comes too late and because Equity only requires proof of the fiduciary relationship and the threat of its breach to act, proof of damage or detriment being traditionally a common law requirement?[16]

Now, the law of defamation is concerned with the telling

14. [1981] A.C. 1096.
15. (1988) 82 A.L.R. 1.
16. For a full discussion of these questions see J. Stuckey, "The Equitable Action for Breach of Confidence—Is Information Ever Property?" (1981) 9 (No. 2) Syd. L.R. 401 at pp. 414 *et seq.*

of the truth in the public interest. The law of confidence is concerned with the suppression of true but secret information from publication. There would seem here to be created a potential collision course, particularly in the modern context of investigative journalism which seeks to reveal and comment upon the secrets of both individuals and corporations, on the one hand, and the government on the other. Certainly in the last 20 years there have been two important developments in this area. One relates to the context in which the law operates, namely, changes in the role and function of the media in contemporary society, and the second relates to the substantive developments in the law of confidentiality itself.

The first change relates to the role of the press. In the eighteenth and nineteenth centuries the press sought to publish freely its opinion on facts which were more or less known to its readers.[17] In the twentieth century the press in Harold Evans' phrase is "half-free".[18] The law in the eighteenth and nineteenth centuries saw that the press was free to express opinion just as individuals were free to express opinions, but in the twentieth century the press in its capacity as voluntary agent of the people's "right to know" can only perform that agency efficiently if it is free as well to publish the facts, the evidence upon which its opinions are formed, and against the background of which the people, its readers, might form their own opinions and judge the cogency of the opinions expressed by the press. The law of confidentiality stands in the way of the press's desire to publish secret facts in many circumstances.

The second change is that the law of confidentiality has been developed and refined in the last 20 years as a necessary protection against unjustifiably intrusive investigative journalism and industrial espionage. Its central concern is to protect the privacy interests of individuals and commercial entities and the security interests of governments. There is clearly no equivalent to the *Bonnard* v. *Perryman* principle in the law of confidentiality.

17. Siebert, *Freedom of the Press in England 1476–1776* (1952).

18. As he explains in his lecture entitled "The Half-Free Press", Granada Guildhall Lectures (1974) at p. 37: "We have a press which is half-free, I believe, because its needs and the needs of the society it serves have outgrown a philosophy rooted in the simpler virtues of free expression. Reality today requires ethical justification for free enquiry and for unimpeded publication of fact rather than opinion."

Indeed it would be odd if there were an exact equivalent. The action protects secret disclosures, prevents publication of information never intended to enter the public domain; all the harm done to the plaintiff lies in the very act of publication and the available remedies post-disclosure are inadequate recompense certainly in cases of disclosure of personal and governmental secrets.[19]

Further difficulties have arisen because an action developed as a private law action is now regularly being invoked in the public law arena to restrain publication of governmental or bureaucratic secrets: as in *Commonwealth* v. *Fairfax*[20] and the various *Spycatcher* cases.[21] The proper view is that in circumstances where it is the press which seeks to publish confidential information as voluntary agent of public's right to know about the functioning of government or other properly public matters, the principle of freedom of speech should be recognised in a substantive way as it is in the law of defamation. On the other hand, where the secret sought to be published is of a personal biographical nature or a trade secret, the private equitable right to confidentiality ought to be pre-eminent. It should be a source of some national pride that the Australian courts embrace this view far more satisfactorily than the English and in the bureaucratic and governmental secrecy context, more satisfactorily even than the American courts. This effective approximation to the *Bonnard* v. *Perryman* rule is found in the application of the so-called "defence" of disclosure in the public interest in the context of governmental secrecy, and in the context of personal and trade secrets, in the ordinary applications of equitable discretion to refuse equitable relief on the basis of the plaintiff's unclean hands. It is convenient, for the purposes of discussion, to divide the cases into those concerned with governmental secrecy and those concerned with personal and trade secrets.

Injunctions to prevent disclosure of governmental secrets

The first case in which the private equitable action for breach of confidence was involved in what is properly a public law

19. *Supra* fn. 16 at pp. 430–432.
20. 147 C.L.R. 39; 32 A.L.R. 485.
21. Especially relevant to this discussion are the decisions reported at [1988] 2 W.L.R. 805 (Court of Appeal); [1988] 3 W.L.R. 776 (House of Lords).

context was the case of *Attorney-General* v. *Jonathan Cape.*[22] The Attorney-General applied for an injunction to restrain the publication of diaries kept by a deceased Labour Cabinet Minister, Lord Crossman. These dealt in some detail with cabinet discussions, deliberation of government committees and advice received from civil servants. Revelations concerned matters which had occurred some 10 to 11 years before the proposed publication. Lord Widgery took the view that disclosure would not undermine the relationship of confidence which existed between current government ministers. However, he did comment that he would have granted the injunction if the publication had followed soon after the relevant cabinet meetings. The judge places particular emphasis in his judgment upon the importance of free speech in respect of government secrets.

In Australia in 1980, Mason J., as he then was, was called upon to adjudicate in relation to government secrecy and confidentiality in the case of *Commonwealth of Australia* v. *John Fairfax.*[23] In that case the Commonwealth sought to restrain the publication of sections from a book entitled *Documents on Australian Defence and Foreign Policy 1968–75* in which secret government documents were reproduced. Mason J. refused to grant the injunction on the basis of breach of confidence though he was prepared to grant the injunction on the basis of breach of copyright. In relation to the breach of confidence argument, he said that he refused to grant an injunction to restrain a publication in breach of confidence which disclosed revelations which were merely embarrassing to the government in the conduct of its foreign policies. He took an opportunity to outline the general principles which operate in this area and indeed placed the onus on the government to establish that a sufficient detriment to citizens would be brought about if the secret information were disclosed:

> "The Court will not prevent the publication of information which merely throws light on the past workings of government, even if it be not public property so long as it does not prejudice the community in other respects. Then disclosure will itself serve the public interest in keeping the community informed and in promoting discussion of public affairs. If, however, it appears that disclosure will be inimicable

22. [1976] Q.B. 752.
23. *Supra* fn. 20.

to the public interest because national security, relations with foreign countries or the ordinary business of government will be prejudiced, disclosure will be restrained. There will be cases in which the conflicting considerations will be finely balanced, where it is difficult to decide whether the public interest in knowing and in expressing its opinion outweighs the need to protect confidentiality."[24]

He considered it was for the government to establish detriment before the publication would be enjoined, enunciating a presumption against prior restraint unless irreparable damage to the polity could be shown to be the inevitable result of publication.

He found support for his approach in the views of Widgery L.J. in the *Crossman Diaries* case.[25] The principle so elaborated by Mason J. is particularly well adapted to the problem of reconciling the public interest in freedom of information with the need for confidentiality in the bureaucratic and governmental context. The "iniquity rule" which operates in cases relating to the disclosure of private and trade secrets has no place here.[26] A different, and necessarily broader concept of public interest such as was enunciated by Mason J. is required.

It is instructive to compare the approach of Mason J. with the more politically conservative approach of the House of Lords in *British Steel Corporation* v. *Granada*.[27] In that case an employee of BSC had breached his duty of confidence by disclosing to Granada Television documents which revealed BSC's internal mismanagement as well as government intervention during a national steel strike. The action was bought by BSC to force Granada to disclose the name of their informant and Granada accepted that the disclosure was a breach of confidence and relied upon the alleged immunity from disclosure of press sources. The House of Lords considered that the legitimate interest of the public in knowing about the affairs of the statutory corporation in question was adequately satisfied through the restricted and admittedly general information which was published by the Secretary of State annually. Lord Wilberforce said: "That some of the internal activities of BSC at particular times are of interest to the public there can be no doubt. But there

24. 32 A.L.R. at p. 493.
25. See fn. 22.
26. The "iniquity rule" is discussed at pages 152–157, *infra*.
27. [1981] A.C. 1096; [1981] 1 All E.R. 417.

is a wide difference between what is interesting to the public and what it is in the public interest to know."[28]

Lord Salmon, on the other hand, in a strong dissent stressed the need for the press to be free to publish fact as well as opinion in relation to issues of national economic and political consequence such as this.

Certainly the BSC employee had acted undoubtedly out of a sincere concern for what was going on in one of Britain's main nationalised industries and on the principles which Mason J. outlined, a different decision may well have been reached in Australia.[29]

Finally, and in conclusion, very recently, in the final judgment of the House of Lords in the *Spycatcher* saga in *Attorney-General* v. *Guardian Newspapers Ltd.*,[30] the House of Lords has ultimately approved the approach of Mason J. in *Commonwealth* v. *Fairfax*.[31] The onus must be on the Crown to prove detriment to public interest before such an injunction will be granted to restrain a breach of confidence.[32]

At least until recent times the law in the United States afforded a complete contrast. No proceedings to restrain the publication of government information seem to have been taken before the *Pentagon Papers* case in 1971.[33] In that case, the U.S. Government requested an order to restrain publication in the *New York Times* and the *Washington Post* of secret State Department compilations of papers relating to United States' involvement in the Vietnam War. The Supreme Court refused to order the prior restraint. With the exception of Marshall J., the majority regarded the prior restraint issue as decisive. While two judges took the view that the First Amendment wholly precludes any prior restraint of any kind, the view of the majority was best expressed in the dictum of Stuart J., that an injunction will only

28. [1981] 1 All E.R. at p. 455.

29. There is an interesting and exhaustive discussion of this case in V.T. Bevan, "The Recent Decline and Fall of Freedom of the Press in English Law" [1983] 16 *Vanderbilt Journal of Transnational Law* 31–52.

30. *Supra* fn. 21.

31. *Supra* fn. 20.

32. [1988] 3 W.L.R. 776 at pp. 785–786 (*per* Lord Keith of Kinkel) and at pp. 807–808 (*per* Lord Goff).

33. *Supra* fn. 2.

issue if: "Disclosure will surely result in direct, immediate and irreparable damage to our Nation or its people."[34].

All members of the majority were influenced by the absence of any Congressional statute authorising the granting of an injunction in these circumstances and formulated a more severe test for the validity of a prior restraint in this context than that employed in other kinds of prior restraint cases.[35]

However, the Federal District Court in *U.S.* v. *Progressive Incorporated*[36] granted an injunction to restrain publication of an article which described in technical detail the manufacture of the H-Bomb. On the basis of expert evidence the judge found that the information thus disclosed might enable a medium power country to make the bomb more expeditiously and concluded that there was more justification for the government's view that publication would endanger national security than there had been in the *Pentagon Papers* case.[37] Finally, in *Snepp* v. *U.S.*,[38] the Supreme Court upheld as constitutional a relevant contractual provision requiring agents employed by the CIA to submit any forthcoming publication for preliminary clearance by the CIA. It also imposed a constructive trust for the government's benefit over the profits from the sale of the defendant's book which had not in fact been submitted for clearance in breach of contract. The majority paid scant regard to the prior restraint issue. A term requiring submission for approval of all material, whether classified or not, certainly inhibits speech which is constitutionally protected, and should only be enforced if relevant disclosures would create a serious risk of direct and irreparable damage to the nation. Nevertheless, the case was treated somewhat inexplicably as a case essentially about contractual obligation.[39]

34. *Ibid.*
35. *Supra* fn. 3.
36. 467 F. Supp. 990 (1979).
37. *Supra* fn. 1.
38. 444 U.S. 507 (1980).
39. There is an excellent analysis of these cases in Eric Barendt, *Freedom of Speech* (Oxford, 1985).

Injunctions to prevent disclosure of personal or trade secrets

The English approach

In these cases, the approach which the Enlgish courts have adopted is significantly different from that of the Australian courts. The English courts undertake a subjective King Solomon-like "balancing of competing public interests" exercise in order to determine whether an injunction restraining publication will be granted. All relevant "public interests" are argued for and considered. Certainly, no pre-eminence is accorded to the public interest in confidentiality or the principle of freedom of expression or of the press. Each case is determined on its merits.

The origin of this approach is said to be found in *Gartside* v. *Outram*.[40] The plaintiff employer attempted to prevent a former employee from disclosing his fraudulent business dealings. In refusing the injunction, Wood V.-C. said in a classic dictum:

> "There is no confidence as to the disclosure of iniquity. You cannot make me a confidant of a crime or fraud and be entitled to close up my lips upon any secret which you have the audacity to disclose to me relating to any fraudulent intention on your part: such a confidence cannot exist."[41]

The English courts have interpreted the case as authority for the development of a "public interest defence" which involves adjudicating upon the balance of competing public interests. It goes beyond the unclean hands defence in Equity and is more like the legal plea of justification in defamation.

The modern statement of the "iniquity rule" is found in Lord Denning's judgment in *Initial Services Limited* v. *Putterill*.[42] This was a case involving the English restrictive trade practices legislation. The first defendant had been the sales manager of the plaintiff launderers. When he resigned he took with him several of the plaintiff's confidential documents which he gave to the second defendant, a national newspaper. Relying on the information in these documents and on further information which the first defendant gave them, the newspaper published an article alleging that the plaintiffs in breach of that legislation

40. (1857) 26 L.J. Ch. 113.
41. *Ibid.* at p. 114.
42. [1968] 1 Q.B. 396.

had misled their customers by saying that increases in their charges were caused not by these agreements but by the government's selective employment tax. The defence was upheld by the Court of Appeal. Lord Denning discussed the "iniquity rule" and said that he did not think that it was confined simply to cases where the employer had been guilty of a crime or fraud. He said:

"I do not think that it is so limited. It extends to any misconduct of such a nature that it ought, in public interest, to be disclosed to others. The exception should extend to crimes, frauds and misdeeds, both those actually committed as well as those in contemplation provided always and this is essential that the disclosure is justified in the public interest. The reason is because no private obligations can dispense with that universal one which lies on every member of the society to discover every design which may be formed contrary to the laws of society to destroy the public welfare."[43]

Lord Denning went on to say that the disclosure should be made to one who had a proper interest in receiving the information. Thus in the present case it would be proper to disclose the fraud to the police or breach of the Restrictive Trade Practices Act to the registrar, but he considered also that there may be cases where the misdeed is of such a character that the public interest may demand or at least excuse publication on a broad field even to the press. Lord Denning did not think in these circumstances publication to or by the press was justified. Lord Denning took a similar view in *Fraser* v. *Evans*,[44] a case in which the court found that the plaintiff had no standing to complain of a breach of confidence by the *Sunday Times* publishing the confidential material which the plaintiff had prepared under contract to the Greek Government. In *Hubbard* v. *Vosper*[45] the claim of the famous scientology leader to the confidentiality of the material contained in his courses was rejected on the basis that the courses were inherently dangerous even to the extent of being capable of causing physical injury. It was therefore in the public interest that the contents should be made known. The Court of Appeal spoke exclusively in terms of balancing the public interest in disclosure, that is, balancing the principle of freedom of expression against that of the public

43. *Ibid.* at pp. 405–406.
44. [1969] 1 Q.B. 349.
45. [1972] 2 Q.B. 84.

interest in preserving confidences rather than in terms of the "iniquity" rule. In *Beloff* v. *Pressdram*[46] the judge discussed the public interest exception as applied by the court in *Hubbard* v. *Vosper*.[47] Ungoed-Thomas J. said:

"The defence of public interest clearly covers and in the authorities does not extend beyond disclosure which as Lord Denning M.R. emphasised must be disclosure justified in the public interest. These are matters carried out or contemplated in breach of the country's security or in breach of law, including statutory duty, fraud or otherwise destructive for the country or its people including matters medically dangerous to the public and other misdeeds of a similar gravity. Public interest, as a defence in law operates to override the rights of the individual, including copyright which would prevail and which the law is also concerned to protect. Such public interest as now recognised by the law, does not extend beyond misdeeds of a serious nature and importance to the country and thus in my view clearly recognisable as such."[48]

In 1977 Lord Denning decided the case of *Woodward* v. *Hutchins*.[49] In that case, a pop group sought to prevent the publication of newspaper articles based upon salacious stories revealed by their ex-manager. The plaintiffs also issued a libel writ against the defendants and the defendants intended to plead justification. Lord Denning rejected their claim for injunctive relief on the basis that there was an overriding public interest in disclosure:

"If a group of this kind seeks publicity which is to their advantage it seems to me that they cannot complain if a servant or employee of theirs afterwards discloses the truth about them. If the image which they fostered is not a true image it is in the public interest that it should be corrected. In these cases it is a question of balancing the public interest in maintaining confidence against the public interest in knowing the truth. In this case the balance comes down in favour of the truth being told even if it should involve some breach of confidential information."[50]

Lord Lawton agreed, and held that since the claim in defamation was interwoven with the claim in confidentiality, no injunction would be granted.

46. [1973] 1 All E.R. 241.
47. *Supra* fn. 43.
48. *Supra* fn. 46 at p. 260.
49. [1977] 1 W.L.R. 760.
50. *Ibid* at pp. 763–764.

Similarly, the judgments in more recent English cases certainly show little inclination to give any pre-eminence to either the principle of freedom of the press or the fiduciary confidential relationship in the "balancing of public interest" exercise.

In *Schering Chemicals* v. *Falkman*[51] a drug company employed a firm of media consultants to train some of its executives to counteract adverse publicity resulting from the defects of one of its drug products. The defendant Elstein had been employed by the firm to conduct a training course for the drug company executives. Ten years later he prepared a film for Thames Television about the drug and its alleged harmful effects. A majority of the Court of Appeal granted the drug company an injunction to restrain broadcasting of the film on the ground of breach of confidence. Lord Justice Templeman did not think the order interfered with press freedom. The film, he said, could still be made and shown but Elstein, bound by a duty of confidence, could not assist in its preparation. It seems, however, probable from the readings of the case that both Templeman and Shaw L.JJ. would have granted the injunction even if it did have the effect of preventing fresh information about the drug from reaching the public. Lord Denning's dissent emphasised the undesirability of imposing any prior restraint in this situation. Following the approach of the European Court of Justice in the *Sunday Times* contempt case[52] he urged that disclosure of information of public interest should not be prevented on the ground of breach of confidence unless there is a pressing social need for the confidence to be preserved.[53]

In *Francome* v. *Mirror Group Newspapers*[54] an interlocutory injunction was granted to restrain the publication by a newspaper of an article based on the tapes of illegally taped telephone conversations which revealed alleged breaches of the rules of racing by the plaintiff. The Master of the Rolls, Sir John Donaldson, disparaged the defendant's freedom of the press argument. In these circumstances, he held, the public interest could be best served by sending the tapes to the police or the Jockey Club and that disclosure on a wide field was not justified. Contrast

51. [1982] Q.B. 1.
52. (1979) 2 E.H.R.R. 245.
53. *Supra* fn. 29 at pp. 55–57.
54. [1984] 1 W.L.R. 892.

this to the decision in *Lion Laboratories* v. *Evans*[55] where a differently composed Court of Appeal lifted an injunction which had been granted to restrain publication in the press of an article based upon information in documents disclosed to the newspaper by former employees of the plaintiff alleging defects in a breathalyser machine made by the plaintiff and used by the police. The Court of Appeal considered that the public interest in the accuracy of the machine, the proper administration of justice in this case, overrode any private right of confidence.

The Australian approach

By way of contrast, the Australian courts have never embraced the "balancing of public interest" approach and have consistently taken the view that in cases where an injunction to protect a personal or trade secret is sought, the equitable right to confidentiality should be given pre-eminence unless the plaintiff comes to the court with unclean hands or there is some other factor disentitling the plaintiff to equitable relief.

The "balancing of public interest" approach taken by the English courts in the interpretation of the defence was severely criticised by Rath J. in the case of *Castrol* v. *Em-Tech Associates*.[56] He criticised the approach for its underlying assumption that there is some kind of equality between all the arguable relevant public interests. He says: "If Lord Denning's quoted statement is taken literally the court will test the legitimacy of breach of confidence by its conception of the balance of public interest in the particular circumstances of the case. As in *Woodward* v. *Hutchins* itself the balance may weigh down in favour of disclosure even if no iniquity, either criminal or tortious, is involved."[57] He goes on to say: "In my opinion the court in considering whether just case for breaking confidence exists must have regard to matters of a more weighty and precise kind than a public interest in the truth being told."[58]

55. [1984] 3 W.L.R. 539.
56. (1981) 33 A.L.R. 31.
57. *Ibid.* at p. 56.
58. *Ibid.*

Similarly, in *TPC* v. *Allied Mills*[59], *G.* v. *Day*[60] and *G.M.H.* v. *David Syme*,[61] the Australian courts have refused to adopt the English approach and have preferred to protect the fiduciary relationship of confidence once established, so long as the secret is one which Equity in its discretion ought to protect and the plaintiff comes to Equity with clean hands. If it is not, of course, disclosure to others is sanctioned, and any remedy for damage done by publication must sound in defamation or on some other ground.

Very recently, the Australian approach has found scholarly vindication. In his judgment in *Corrs Pavey Whitting* v. *Collector of Customs*,[62] Gummow J. provides a close analysis of the leading early authority of *Gartside* v. *Outram*[63] which shows that it does not provide any basis for the English "balancing of public interest" approach. He points out that the decision in that case is based on the fact that any court of law or equity would have been extremely unlikely to imply into a contract between master and servant an obligation that servant's good faith to his master required him to keep secret details of his master's gross bad faith to his customers; or that, even if the plaintiffs had valid legal rights they would have been denied relief, on general equitable principles, because of unclean hands. Thus, the judge properly defines the ambit of the so-called defence as being simply an illustration of the operation of equitable discretion:

> "information will lack the necessary attribute of confidence if the subject matter is the existence or real likelihood of the existence of any iniquity in the sense of a crime, civil wrong or serious misdeed of public importance, and the confidence is relied upon to prevent disclosure to a third party with a real and direct interest in redressing such crime, wrong or misdeed."[64]

59. 34 A.L.R. 105.
60. [1982] 1 N.S.W.L.R. 24.
61. [1984] N.S.W.L.R. 294.
62. 74 A.L.R. 428.
63. *Supra* fn. 40.
64. *Supra* fn. 62 at p. 450.

SHOULD AN INTERLOCUTORY INJUNCTION BE GRANTED ON ANOTHER GROUND EVEN THOUGH ONE HAS BEEN REFUSED ON THE GROUND OF DEFAMATION OR BREACH OF CONFIDENTIALITY?

In the governmental secrecy context

Where the press seeks to disclose governmental information and the facts are both true and obtained in breach of confidence, but the publication is justified in the public interest, should the plaintiff still be able to restrain that publication if the press seeks to reproduce that information in a form which breaches the plaintiff's copyright? The legitimate demands of modern investigative journalism as agent of the public's "right to know" may require the provision of "the evidence", usually in the form of the reproduction of a leaked document. This was one of the issues in *Commonwealth* v. *Fairfax*.[65]

The inconsistency of Mason J.'s judgment in *Commonwealth* v. *Fairfax*[66] is found in his granting an injunction on the basis of infringement of copyright in the leaked documents, a clear fetter on freedom of expression. He was not prepared to enforce a public interest defence to breach of copyright, analogous to that which operated in respect of the breach of governmental confidence claim.

Is there an analogous defence to the public interest justification in defamation and confidence to be found in the law of copyright? There are three possibilities:

1. section 41 of the Copyright Act 1968 (Cth);
2. section 42 of the Act; and
3. a common law public interest defence.

These three possibilities were discussed by Mason J. Section 41 provides a defence relating to a fair dealing with the plaintiff's documents for the purpose of criticism and review provided that a sufficient acknowledgement of the work is made. It is an accepted principle of copyright law that the publication of a hitherto unpublished work could never be "fair" since it was a publication without the consent of the author as was held

65. *Supra* fn. 20.
66. *Ibid.*

in *British Oxygen Co.* v. *Liquid Air Ltd.*[67] Certainly a surreptitious acquisition of the author's work cannot base a "fair" dealing. On the other hand, the purpose of the publication in cases like *Commonwealth* v. *Fairfax* is to publicise the information contained in the work rather than to criticise or review the manner and style of the literary form in which that information is presented. Parliament could not have intended this defence to have any relevance to the circumstance in which a leaked document is published in order that the information which it discloses may be authenticated, criticised and reviewed rather than so that its "literary form" may be criticised and reviewed.

Mason J. did consider, however, that a dealing with unpublished works which would be unfair as against an author who is a private individual may nevertheless be considered "fair" as against a government, if that dealing simply promotes public knowledge and public discussion of government action. Just because the contemporary role of the press as provider of information to the public did not fall within the contemplation of the draftsman of the Copyright Act does not mean that the courts could not construe these sections in such a way. Mason J. said however that it would not be appropriate for him on the interlocutory application before him to proceed on the footing that such a construction will ultimately prevail.

Section 42 provides that there may be a fair dealing with a literary work for the purpose of or associated with the reporting of news in a newspaper if a sufficient acknowledgement of the work is made. News may not be restricted to current events. Still section 42, while it was not available in *Commonwealth* v. *Fairfax*,[68] may be useful in circumstances where the press is seeking to publish the information in a "literary work" as news.

Finally, the common law public interest defect. This issue was first discussed in the English case of *Beloff* v. *Pressdram*.[69] In that case the plaintiff sought to restrain the publication of a secret internal office memorandum written by her which the defendant sought to publish after obtaining it surreptitiously. The case was framed in copyright and failed on the basis that

67. [1925] Ch. 383.
68. *Supra* fn. 20.
69. [1973] 1 All E.R. 241 at p. 260; see discussion *supra* p. 12.

the plaintiff, as the employee of a paper for which she wrote, was not the owner of the copyright in the memorandum and the subsequent purported assignment to her of the copyright was not valid. The trial judge took the view that there *was* a defence of public interest which was distinct from that of fair dealing within the English equivalents to sections 41 and 42. He considered that the scope of this defence was analogous to the scope of the public interest defence in breach of confidence but since the information disclosed did not relate to misdeeds of a serious nature such as breaches of national security, or of law, fraud, or matters destructive of the country or public health and safety, the defence was inapplicable in that case.

Mason J. supports this view:

> "It makes legitimate the publication of confidential information or material in which copyright subsists so as to protect the community from destruction, damage or harm. The defence applies to disclosures of things done in breach of national security and breach of law including fraud and to disclosure of matters which involve danger to the public. So far there is no recorded instance of the defence having been raised in a case such as this where the suggestion is that the advice given by Australia's public servants particularly its diplomats should be ventilated with a view to exposing what it alleged to have been the pursuit of expedient goals especially in relation to East Timor. To apply the defence to such a situation would break new ground."[70]

He refused to "break new ground" and considered that the defendants had not persuaded him that it was more likely than not that any of the suggested defences would prevail and so the plaintiff succeeded in the action on the *Beecham* test.[71] The judge granted an interlocutory injunction, on the basis that the plaintiff's copyright in the documents would become less valuable if publication went ahead and really because damages or an account of profits would be inadequate recompense. He said that the plaintiff's copyright would be lessened and on the other hand the real damage to the government caused by public knowledge acquired by disclosures would not be adequately measured in monetary terms. The effect of his decision is that while the injunction was not granted on the breach of confidence ground, it was *de facto* granted: the same effect was achieved on the basis of breach of copyright.

70. 32 A.L.R. at p. 497.
71. *Supra* fn. 13.

Ultimately Mason J. took the view of the authors Laddie, Prescott and Victoria, expressed in their book *The Modern Law of Copyright*, that copyright is purely a creature of statute law and the only public interest defences provided by the Act are of limited scope.[72] Copyright, a right of property, is conferred by a statute and can only be taken away by statute and that is the effect of Mason J.'s judgment in *Commonwealth* v. *Fairfax*.[73] He refuses to break new ground in finding that the public interest in publication of copyright documents belonging to the government could be defended or justified in the public interest as it may be in breach of confidence or defamation. It is the writer's view that he should also have agreed with the final conclusion of the authors and found, that while there is no defence conferred by the Copyright Act 1968 (Cth), on the other hand the public interest becomes relevant at the stage when the court has to decide what remedy is appropriate. In granting an injunction the court may take into account the interests of third parties and the interests of the public as a whole as third parties. Mason J. was not prepared in this case to take the bold step, the revolutionary step, of elevating such a public interest consideration relevant to a grant of remedy into a substantive defence to an action for infringement of copyright where the question related to an interlocutory injunction in restraint of speech. It is the writer's view that he ought so to have done because his conclusion in relation to the copyright infringement claim completely negatived the thesis behind his reasoning in relation to the breach of confidence ground and produced a result which amounted to an equally effective prior restraint. After all, he was prepared to shift the burden of establishing the claim to secrecy on to the government in respect of the breach of confidence claim and find that the government could not justify the preservation of its secrecy in the public interest.

An interesting light was thrown on the relationship between confidentiality and copyright as grounds for injunctive relief in the governmental secrecy context in the final set of *Spycatcher* discussions in the English courts: the Court of Appeal and House of Lords' judgments in *Attorney-General* v. *Guardian*

72. Butterworths, 1980, at para. 2.107, pp. 71–72.
73. See fn. 20.

Newspapers; *Attorney-General* v. *Observer Ltd.* and *Attorney-General* v. *The Times.*[74]

In the action for injunctive relief against *The Times*, the newspaper which had the exclusive rights to serialise Wright's book in the U.K., the injunction granted by the trial judge on the basis of breach of confidence was affirmed in relation to the serialisation of the book which occurred *before* the secrets there disclosed had become public knowledge through extensive international publication. The House of Lords reluctantly confirmed that however treacherous Peter Wright's conduct in writing this book, once the secrets which formed the subject-matter of his lifelong fiduciary duty to the Crown were public knowledge, no injunction against publication of his book could be justified. The duty had lost its substance, its subject-matter, and thus its enforcement would be a useless exercise.

All the judges express their distaste and chagrin at the possibility that Peter Wright would now be free to profit from his conduct by publishing his book in the U.K. Although the Crown, arguing its case solely on the confidentiality ground, had refused to present any arguments on the basis of infringement of Crown copyright, several of the judges in what are admittedly *obiter* comments suggested, indeed threatened, that the English courts ought to refuse to protect or enforce Wright's copyright by way of injunction if he went on to publish his book in the U.K.

In particular, Dillon L.J. in the Court of Appeal considered that the copyright in the book belonged to the Crown and any of Wright's prospective profits would be held on constructive trust for the Crown; and that any other publishers could avail themselves of the defence of fair dealing in the public interest if *The Times* or Wright sought to sue for breach of copyright.[75]

The lack of doctrinal logic in these suggestions is obvious. While Wright may have discovered the secrets, the information, which he disclosed in his manuscript while in the employ of the Crown, he did not write the book as an employee and therefore, the copyright in the work was his, failing the order of a prior restraint on the basis of breach of confidentiality. No more plausible is the suggestion that Wright ought not to be permitted to profit from his wrongdoing, his breach of his duty

74. *Supra* fn. 21.
75. [1988] 2 W.L.R. 805 at p. 899.

of confidence: if no secret remains, there is no remedy for the breach—the injunction is too late.

Lord Justice Dillon's error was perpetuated in the House of Lords' judgment in which four of the five judges (Lords Keith, Brightman, Griffiths and Goff) agreed that the copyright in Peter Wright's book was vested in the Crown in its own right or as beneficiary under a constructive trust. The analysis of Lord Jauncey, however, is preferable: he stresses (as mentioned by Lords Keith, Griffiths and Goff) that while the copyright might be Wright's, the court could refuse to protect his copyright by way of injunction where the copyright work contained false information or was itself immoral.[76] Ironically, the effect of all this could be to encourage wider publication of the government's secrets but it may strip Wright of his profits from exploiting his copyright in the U.K.

Certainly, though, these comments go a long way towards the establishment of a very broad public interest defence at general law to breach of copyright in the U.K., which is analogous to the public interest defence to breach of confidence as expounded in the English courts.[77]

In the private law context

Determinations in the private law context as to whether an injunction will be awarded on another ground, although no injunction would be granted on the ground of defamation, are made with reasonable consistency by the courts. Contemporary Anglo-Australian courts basically and properly take the view that the substantial issue of each case must be addressed to see whether the principle of freedom of expression is fundamental to the case or whether some other principle, for example, the preservation of business goodwill (passing off and malicious falsehood) or the protection of consumers from deceptive or misleading conduct (section 52 of the Trade Practices Act 1974

76. [1988] 3 W.L.R. 776 at pp. 817–818.

77. Note that s. 171(3) of the Copyright Act 1988 (U.K.) states that nothing in the copyright provisions contained in the Act affects any rule of law preventing or restricting the enforcement of copyright, on grounds of public interest or otherwise. There is no equivalent provision in the Australian Copyright Act 1968 (Cth) so that it, unlike in the U.K., remains arguable in Australia that the defences expressly provided in the Act are an exhaustive set.

(Cth)) is pre-eminent. If the principle of freedom of speech is central, then no injunction will lie; if some other principle is essential the prior restraint will operate. The considerations which are relevant to such a decision are admirably canvassed by Hunt J. in the case of *The Church of Scientology of California Incorporated* v. *Readers' Digest Services*[78] in which the judge points out that the pre-eminence will be given to the *Bonnard* v. *Perryman* rule and that only in cases where freedom of expression is a secondary consideration, will a prior restraint upon another ground be available. So, in *Swimsure Laboratories* v. *McDonald*,[79] the plaintiff company had spent a large amount on preliminary promotion of its new product but had not yet placed the product on the market. The defendant had disparaged the product to potential retailers and had falsely asserted that the product had failed to receive Health Commission approval. The defendant claimed he could justify his statements. Hunt J. granted the injunction, on the basis of injurious falsehood, saying that the case was not essentially concerned with the public interest in free expression but rather was one in which a trade rival in maliciously disparaging the plaintiff's goods would cause irreparable damage to the plaintiff's product launch if no injunction were granted.

On the other hand, in *Bestobells Paints* v. *Bigg*,[80] an injunction to restrain a dissatisfied consumer from maintaining a sign on his house walls (which were covered in peeling paintwork) which said "This house is painted with Carson's paint", on the basis of trade mark infringement and in particular, injurious falsehood was refused in the interests of free speech. This was a case, not of a trade rival maliciously disparaging the plaintiff's goods, but of an ordinary citizen asserting his right to free speech, claiming he could justify his claim at final hearing.

In *Woodward* v. *Hutchins*,[81] the Court of Appeal took the view that the case was one which ought to sound in damages for defamation only and would not grant injunctive relief on the independent ground of breach of confidence.[82] The

78. [1980] 1 N.S.W.L.R. 344 at p. 349.
79. [1979] 2 N.S.W.L.R. 796.
80. [1975] 1 F.S.R. 421.
81. [1977] 1 W.L.R. 760.
82. A similar result was reached in the case of *Lennon* v. *News Group Newspapers Ltd.* [1978] F.S.R. 573.

Australian courts would probably have reached a similar conclusion on these facts, not on the subjective "balancing of public interests" approach that there should be truth in advertising or "image" promotion, but on the basis that the plaintiff came to court with unclean hands (the so-called secrets relating to immoral conduct) or that the information itself was mere "gossip" and not worthy of the court's protection.

More recently in Australia, in *Construction Industry Long Service Leave Board* v. *Odco*,[83] the defendant had asserted that a member of the plaintiff Board has been the subject of undue union influence. Interlocutory injunctions were sought to restrain the alleged defamation and the breach of section 52 of the Trade Practices Act 1974 (Cth), found in the misleading and deceptive conduct involved in the making of such imputations. Jenkinson J. refused to grant the interlocutory injunction sought, finding that the applicants had failed to show a serious question to be tried in respect of the allegations of misleading conduct, but he did stress that this was a case in which freedom of expression was a central concern and that even if a serious question to be tried had been shown, no prior restraint would have been available.

The final decision to be discussed in this section is an English one: *News Group Newspapers Ltd.* v. *The Mirror Group*.[84] This case concerned a "knocking advertisement" of the defendants which the plaintiffs sought to enjoin from publication on the basis that it infringed their registered trade mark in the words "the *Sun*" and copyright in their newspaper's masthead and name "the *Sun*". The plaintiff and defendant were rival newspaper proprietors. The defendant published an advertisement the clear implication of which was that the plaintiff's editorial line was uncritical of the government, in which it used the plaintiff's "the *Sun*" masthead under a heading "Yes, Prime Minister" and its own under a heading, "No, Prime Minister". The injunction was granted to restrain publication of the advertisement, although one might justifiably doubt whether the use of the words "the *Sun*" by the defendants was use "as a trade mark" in the manner required for trade mark infringement and whether there was on the facts of the case a relevant protectable copyright

83. 81 A.L.R. 590.
84. [1989] 1 F.S.R. 126.

in the name and decorative masthead. What is worrying about the decision is the failure of the court to advert to freedom of speech considerations in determining the prior restraint issue. After all the litigants were not simple and straightforward trade rivals, but both members of the Fourth Estate and the content of the advertisement was an opinion about political bias in press reporting.

CONCLUSION

This essay has addressed itself to the question of how consistently the contemporary Anglo-Australian courts reconcile due acknowledgement of the principle of freedom of speech with the imposition of prior restraints upon publication by way of interlocutory injunction in cases of defamation, breach of confidence, copyright and in other cases concerning other miscellaneous intellectual property rights and economic torts. It has been illustrated that legal rules which give due recognition to the principle of freedom of speech are enunciated in the cases but their manner of judicial application in any particular case remains relatively unpredictable.

Absent a constitutional protection for freedom of speech, the Anglo-Australian courts are faced each time a prior restraint issue arises with delicate determinations in relation to the exercise of injunctive discretion. The recent recognition in both Australia and the U.K. that the *Bonnard* v. *Perryman* rule in defamation law ought to have an analogous operation in respect of the breaching of governmental confidence is to be applauded but recognition of a similar rule in relation to breach of copyright awaits to be authoritatively determined in both jurisdictions. Until that time, the press, particularly the "investigative" press, remains in Harold Evans' immortal phrase "half-free",[85] free to publish assertion, allegation and opinion but not free to publish the documentary "evidence", which may be necessary to authenticate the facts upon which the particular assertions, allegations and opinions are founded.

JENNIFER STUCKEY-CLARKE

85. *Supra* fn. 18.

INDEX